Strange Stories
From Devon

Rosemary Anne Lauder
& Michael Williams

Bossiney Books

D1465330

First published in 1982
by Bossiney Books
St Teath, Bodmin, Cornwall
Designed, typeset and printed in Great Britain by
Penwell Ltd, Parkwood, Callington
Cornwall

© *1982 Rosemary Anne Lauder*
and Michael Williams

ISBN 0 906456 61 4

PLATE ACKNOWLEDGMENTS

Front cover by David Golby
Pages 7, 9, 11, 96, 97 Richard Isbell
Pages 5, 6, 13, 27, 53, 54, 57, 91 Ray Bishop
Page 14 by courtesy of The Clovelly Estate Company Ltd
Pages 37, 38, 62, 64, 69 by courtesy of Devon and Cornwall
Constabulary
Page 54 Ray Bishop by courtesy of Cecil Cole Ltd
Pages 15, 16, 74, 77, 85, 86 Rosemary Anne Lauder
Page 25 by courtesy of Mrs B. Dickinson
Pages 41, 42, 43, 45, 94 Western Morning News Co. Ltd
Page 19 Joan Rendell
Pages 21, 88 John Jeffery
Page 26 Jeannie Hampshire
Page 59 Bertrand Heath
Page 98 Chris Chapman
Pages 48, 51 John Chard
Page 73 National Monuments Record
Page 31 Paul Honeywill
Page 76 Mill Street Studio

About the Authors — and the Book

Rosemary Anne Lauder moved from Middlesex to North Devon some fifteen years ago and now lives outside Bideford. For several years she has been a regular contributor to the *Bideford Gazette*. Previous titles include three books on North Devon subjects and she is currently working on a book of old Devon photographs.

A Cornishman, Michael Williams started full time publishing in 1975. With his wife Sonia, he runs Bossiney Books from a cottage and converted barn in North Cornwall — they are literally Cornish cottage publishers, specializing in Westcountry subjects by Westcountry authors.

For ten years they ran the Bossiney House Hotel, just outside Tintagel — hence the name Bossiney Books. Then in 1975 they left the hotel business and moved to St Teath. This is their 75th title.

Strange shapes and places — strange characters — the man they couldn't hang, and a Salcombe mystery, the Lynmouth disaster and a mysterious house are some of the strange stories from Devon.

Did King Arthur visit North Devon? Was there really a ghost dog? Who was the bigger rogue — Carew or Froude? A book that poses many intriguing questions.

Strange Shapes — and Places

Devon has her share of strange shapes — and places — her share of impressive landmarks too. Few are more impressive in the whole of the Westcountry than St Michael's Church at Brentor. The shape of tor and church overlooking miles and acres of the Devon landscape poses an inevitable question: 'Why build a church up there?' The simple truth is only the athletic can worship at St Michael's; the slope is steep and there is no road for a car. Shanks's pony is the only way.

The erection of religious edifices on such lofty heights was due to an ancient primitive belief that the raging of a storm was really a conflict between the forces of the Devil and the Heavenly Host. A secondary reason was the attractive idea of sacred buildings, housing holy relics and crosses, keeping evil spirits away from the land below.

Legend also offers an interesting explanation for this church occupying such a bleak, windswept spot. Apparently it was built at the bottom of the tor and dedicated to St Michael; but the Devil, sharply jealous of the Saint, shifted it to the summit. The villagers desperately tried to rebuild the church on its original lower site — but in vain — every time they paused the Devil descended and put it back on top of the tor! Sadly the Devon villagers gave up rebuilding, but they had the wit and wisdom to ask for St Michael's help, and St Michael responded bravely by tackling the Devil in a great wrestling match. Good triumphed over Evil in that St Michael not only won but kicked the Devil down the slope and tossed a huge boulder after him. Today the Church and the boulder remain: two monuments in stone to the legend.

St Michael's, Brentor, 'stands on one of the great ley lines'.▶

Above: St Michael's Church, Brentor: '. . . churches were built along these lines because of a powerful spiritual something'.
Right: 'Dartmoor has some strange faces . . . one of its most famous is Bowerman's Nose.'

Despite its strange isolated geography, men and women have worshipped here on top of this Devon tor for more than eight centuries, and still come here on Sunday evenings in the summer months — the church in the village below is used at other times.

Some old buildings speak to us — provided we have the humility to be quiet and listen. St Michael's has an ability to refresh and renew — and the pamphlet in the church gives us a clue.

'Are you a Christian? Do you believe?

'If you are, then stop. Draw near to God. Pray for us and for yourself. If you are not, we hope that you may stay for a while in this hallowed building where you may discover something of God's majesty and the nearness of his presence.

'So please don't hurry away.'

This Church of St Michael stands on one of the great ley lines, beginning at St Michael's Mount, going through to the Cheesewring on Bodmin Moor, coming here to Brentor on the fringe of Dartmoor,

going on to Somerset to Burrow Mump and Glastonbury, on to Avebury in Wiltshire, further eastward following the approximate course of the Icknield Way, through Bury St Edmunds and finally crossing the coast north of Lowestoft. Or is it finally?

The fact is when we are on these ley lines we are in a region of fascinating speculation and possibility.

Many people are quite convinced that these leys are psychic power centres. Dr Josef Heinsch, a famous German ley hunter, discovered that numerous ancient sites of pagan ceremony and old trackways appeared to link up geometrically. Frequently the Doctor reckoned that Holy lines radiated out from the hills, and churches were built along these lines because of a powerful spiritual something. Maybe the very presence of St Michael's Church perched high above Brentor is such a case.

Certainly the ley hunter, who plots spiritual patterns across the landscape, is on a mystical quest for communion with Mother Earth. As we, twentieth-century searchers, walk these ancient trackways, the spirits of an ancient people and culture somehow touch us. The German Doctor was quite sure this culture was widespread over the planet long, long ago and that modern science will eventually uncover those lost secrets. So curiously by going forward, we shall perhaps be going back.

Who knows but maybe one day the reason for St Michael's lofty presence will be revealed.

★　★　★　★　★

Dartmoor remains a great wilderness. Even today, in some curious way, it can seem as remote as some of the faces of the moon, and Dartmoor has some strange faces, profiles shaped by Nature and Time. One of its most famous is Bowerman's Nose near Manaton.

Sally Jones in her excellent book *Legends of Devon* has written: 'The weathered granite formation is unmistakable, for seen from one angle it resembles the profile of a man with a huge bulbous nose like two potatoes, rearing forty feet above the boulders and outcrops scattered over the slope. As usual the etymologists have a

'These stones on Dartmoor have a good feel . . .'▶

stuffy explanation for the origin of its name, claiming that Bowerman is a corruption of the Celtic *veor maen* or great stone. I prefer the local version, that a man called Bowerman lived at Hound Tor around 1066 and sported a nose identical to the splendidly stubby organ that still adorns the granite column.'

As with St Michael's at Brentor, we enter a field of intriguing speculation. Some people really believed a strange stone structure like this and the Cheesewring on Bodmin Moor were the remains of huge interconnected power storage temples, the Cornish temples being dedicated to the well-being of the body whereas these Devon relations in stone were for revitalizing the spirit.

These stones on Dartmoor have a good feel and you feel better for being there. Some may say that's the natural healing quality of Dartmoor. While others may cynically suggest the power of auto-suggestion. Either way, Bowerman's Nose remains a fascinating shape — a puzzle — and a tonic.

Another fascinating Dartmoor shape is Spinsters' Rock. The only perfect cromlech in all Devon, it stands, as it has done since the megalithic period of prehistory, in a field near that lovely little stannary town of Chagford on the corner of the Moor.

How this strange shape got its name is another Devon puzzle — and it has attracted various theories.

Once more we are back on the subject of ley lines, for this cromlech is said to be on a line from Drewsteignton Church to Throwleigh. Three sturdy upright slabs, seven feet tall, support a gigantic capping stone — and sturdy they must be for that stone weighs sixteen tons. One popular legend is that three spinsters — not single ladies but spinners of yarn — one day spotted stones lying around. Being methodical folk, they gathered up the stones and erected the cromlech. How they got that sixteen-ton stone into position remains a true Devon mystery — like Dartmoor on a misty morning. Another theory is that the word 'Spinsters' is a Gaelic corruption meaning a star-gazing place. A third version is that the stones were carried here by a Moor man and his three sons.

In its time it has been called the Drewsteignton or Shilston Cromlech and it has attracted many visitors, including William Crossing who in his famous *Guide to Dartmoor* in 1912 referred to it as 'a great rock in its bed under Hunt's Tor'. But at least we do know that it is a megalithic burial chamber erected in the second millenium BC.

On this journey among some of the strange shapes which people the Devon landscape, we decided to visit one of the stone circles. Our next destination then was to the Nine Stones or Nine Maidens near Belstone. Legend has it that they dance at twelve noon. Our visit coincided with that apparently magical hour, but alas there was no movement. People, in earlier generations, were quite convinced that such stones moved of their own accord, without human or mechanical aid. Maybe their reluctance today has something to do with twentieth century cynicism.

The fact remains these stones are clusters of atoms and molecules — just as we are — and who knows perhaps as our human bodies renew parts maybe these ancient stones do the same. So when we talk of 'growing stones' or 'moving stones' we are quite possibly clutching at the last remains of an ancient knowledge — in the area of earth currents and their effect on stones.

History curiously can tell us next to nothing about this lovely circle by the village of Belstone. Men and women, down the ages, have made various suggestions as to their original purpose: monu-

Spinsters' Rock: '. . . the only perfect cromlech in Devon'.

ments or temples or areas for astrologers are just some of the ideas, but despite scholarly research, the stones retain their secret defying all certain human explanation.

Visiting them we felt, in some curious almost mystical way, that we were in touch with 'the old people'. Again the cynic may scoff, but we have heard of people suffering a tingling sensation like a mild electric shock when touching parts of a stone circle.

Personally, we can offer no cast-iron explanation for these grey weather-beaten stones — a meeting place, religious perhaps, is probably a reasonable bet. But it is this very mystery which adds to their magnetism.

Moreover we strongly recommend a visit to this and any other stone circles inhabiting the Westcountry for two good reasons. Apart from the fact that they are to be found in some of the remoter regions, provided we can be still and humble — through them — we can pick up echoes from the long ago. Secondly, we recommend an ancient ritual: walk around the circle nine times in a clockwise direction. The old people did this firmly believing it ensured good luck and protection from ill-wishing.

The most remote corner of North Devon is Hartland — the farthest from railways it was once called — and it is at Hartland Point that the Bristol Channel meets the rough, grey Atlantic Ocean. Hartland and its neighbour Clovelly are high, bleak and windswept and on one of the highest and most windswept points is an earthwork of great antiquity, Clovelly Dykes. The modern trunk road, the A39 carrying its stream of holidaymakers, passes within feet of this ancient North Devon site.

The fort, covering an area of over twenty acres, is generally attributed to the Iron Age but one local historian preferred to believe that the great King Arthur himself raised the banks and mounds.

Post-Roman history of North Devon is largely conjecture but the land was occupied by the Dumnonii tribe of whom Arthur was

Belstone Circle : 'We can offer no cast-iron explanation for these
grey weather-beaten stones . . . It is this very
mystery that adds to their magnetism.'▶

reputedly the king. Perhaps they used Clovelly Dykes as their stronghold and meeting place in the north of Devon. Close by are two coastal forts, also of Iron Age date — Embury Beacon on the Atlantic coast, and Windbury on the Bristol Channel coast; possibly look-outs for the larger inland defences. The Reverend Sabine Baring-Gould, that keen historian, wrote of the Dykes nearly a century ago:

'Clovelly Dykes are the largest series of embankments forming a camp in Devon. History is absolutely silent concerning them. They have been somewhat interfered with about what was probably the entrance by a road being cut through them and by the construction of a farm and its outbuildings. Consequently the plan of the entrance cannot be definitely determined.

'As far as can be judged it was raised in the Iron Age, which began about BC 800, but it may have been and probably was occupied in times of war and trouble to a much later period. In fact, iron cannon balls of the times of the Commonwealth have been found in and about it. That the original constructors of the camp employed slings has been abundantly proved by the discovery of great

Clovelly Dykes in 1956 when the centre enclosure was used as a football pitch—you can see the goal posts.

**Tangled undergrowth conceals the ditches of
this Iron Age hillfort.**

numbers of rounded pebbles used as sling-stones. That they also
employed flint for weapons and tools is probable, for although no
flint weapons or arrow heads have been found yet a certain number
of flint flakes have been unearthed, flakes struck off from nodules of
silex brought from Dorset, in the construction of tools or weapons of
that material. Flint would not have been brought there from a
distance except for that purpose, or for use in striking lights, and
the flints found were certainly not hit off in fire kindling. They were
of the character usually discovered where there was a manufacture
of flint arrow heads. Flint was employed for this purpose all through
the Bronze Age and also in that of Iron.

'The defenders of the camp dug holes in the ground and made fires
in these. During the recent exploration one of these fire holes was
discovered full of charcoal. One of the most valuable relics of an

15

Snow-covered Clovelly Dykes in January 1982.

early age for determining the period to which a camp belongs is the pottery. But in excavating at Clovelly Dykes, singularly little was unearthed. Nearer the surface than the original floor were fragments, indeed, but all comparatively modern. The recent excavation of the camp was very barren of results. This is due to the fact that for centuries the area within the Dykes has been ploughed and reploughed so that the soil has been turned over and over again. The moats must have been very deep and the banks considerably higher than they are at present. In one moat, the bottom was not reached though a trench was sunk six feet below the present surface. It was found that to form the moat the rock had been cut through. Undoubtedly the top of the banks was originally further protected by a stout palisade of wood. Though no relics of this palisade were found at Clovelly Dykes, remains of one have been unearthed, charred by fire in other and similar camps.'

The fort consists of a double enclosure, roughly square, surrounded by two banks between fifteen and twenty five feet in height, and deep ditches one of which is partly full of water. There is a large semi-circular enclosure on the east and three rectangular enclosures on the west. Exploring the Dykes is somewhat like wandering round a maze and only from the air can the true design be appreciated.

But the site is magnificent. From the top of the central mounds the view is uninterrupted as far as the eye can see in all directions—across Bideford Bay to Exmoor, inland to Dartmoor, down the coast to Cornwall and Bodmin Moor. No better site could possibly exist in North Devon. At a time when most of the rest of Devon was covered by dense woodland, was this the gathering place of the clans, or a defended settlement where stock could be reared?

Or did King Arthur long, long ago stand aloft gazing out over his kingdom dreaming and planning of one united land?

With that Arthurian possibility in mind, we consulted Barney Camfield who works with psycho-expansion groups in the Westcountry, members of whom claim to have not only lived in Arthurian times but to have been well-known Arthurian characters.

Here anyway are some of their findings. Through regression, a relaxed state of heightened consciousness, three Arthurian characters definitely claim that North Devon is indeed King Arthur Country, too.

Gereint at Clovelly Dykes

This was the 'Arbenni' tribal region during the time of Arthur. It was a tribal settlement area — a defensible enclosure. It seems that it was certainly begun during the Iron Age as easily built-up natural defences. About 440 AD Arben, leader of the Arbenni built up the defences — sea on all other sides to keep away invaders (Saxons it seems). Also there was sporadic trouble from the tribes on Exmoor and the Welsh although they usually attacked from the sea.

You'll see a line up the Tamar Valley and there was a power line — ley line from St Michael's Island up through the valley to Lundy. On Lundy there was a Druidic- Mithraic- Christine religious settlement but Arben and Mellion, the local Bishop (Merlin), decided that Gereint, son of Arben, would be better served by being initiated and trained at the southern end at St Michael's Christine Settlement.

Gereint, led the tribe, but was subservient to Arturos. He was very badly injured in the leg during the fighting, resigned completely as leader of the Arbenii and gave Arthur complete jurisdiction over the Northern Dumnonic area. Gereint became a religious. Arthur divided the lands into three giving the central part including the dykes to Ragnar, Gereint's brother, land to the east to Morgana and that to the south to Morwenna (Morwenstowe).

Came across some interesting factors concerning religious rite at the head of the River Tamar. Very similar to Egyptian and Greek rites.

Morgana 358 BC

A high hill with a flat top rising out of woodlands. There were two banks on the outer edge, with a ditch between them. Inside these was a semicircular raised bank with seven standing stones on it facing towards the sea. In front of this semicircle of stones was a tall four-sided obelisk with a pointed top. Four men in white robes came up to the obelisk and stood one on either side with their backs to the stone. It looked as if it was made of polished granite.

I went higher and looked down on the scene, and could see the force lines (Ley Lines) coming from a great distance, passing through each standing stone in the semicircle and meeting at the obelisk.

Arthur — first attempt tuning in to area:

Arturus was here around 486 AD. Spent a very cold winter, and a summer in the vicinity having moved up from Cornwall. Saw a great number of men who were short in stature with dark hair and dark ruddy complexions, all engaged in digging. They were extending huge ditches, and so encompassing a much larger area than had previously been used as a stronghold of some sort. There were a lot of large buildings within the ditched line forming a community — a large village perhaps would describe it. Some were made of stone which were older, but most were of wood.

The 'feeling' for Arturus was that he was very much a visitor, yet this place was one of a number in the South West which were tribal headquarters. It felt to him like a 'collecting point'.

Observing the area, I saw a massive standing stone on Hartland Point. I was drawn to a system of ley lines which joined Lundy Island with St Michael's Island and when looking at the map afterwards I see that this follows the line of the River Tamar, which seems rather interesting. The next tuning in point on the north coast was at Tintagel, and further down at a point near the estuary

18

'I was drawn to a system of ley lines which joined Lundy Island (above) with St Michael's Island . . .'

of the River Camel. From what I remember of the North Devon coast in this life, Hartland Point commands a great view westwards of the coastline. Arturus seems to spend some time looking out from this cliff top. The area is greatly wooded fairly near to the coastline. My attention was also drawn to another great stone standing on a high point or hill which seemed due south-west of Clovelly Dykes, and south-east from Hartland Point.

2nd attempt:
This time as soon as I 'went in', a lovely red crystal hovered in front of me. This means that at this time there must have been a battle imminent when extra 'power' was required. (As I understand it.)

Into Arthur and he is being very much the leader making firm outlines for increasing defences and he seems to be ranging around the whole area getting to know the lie of the land. He holds the terrain and map in his mind.

There appear the '7', three of whom I recognise as Morgana, Morwenna, and Percival. Arthur seems to be at variance with what they tell him, for he wants to be sure of something that is to happen. Nevertheless they are there to help him.

There is organisation of tribes. The centre of Devon is avoided and travel from south to north was through the Tamar valley, and vice versa. Tribes here seem a 'law unto themselves' was the message.

There was a ceremony on the top of a hill which involved myself and others who were fighting men. Swords were passed through the flames of a huge fire — a purifying process. After this there was another ceremony at the rising place of the Tamar. Also a sort of purifying involving water. This place regarded with reverence. They had a great respect for natural forces. I can tell only by the feeling and seriousness of Arthur at these times.

Another ley-line to Dunkery Beacon. I questioned the use of islands as 'power centres' from where the ley systems seem to fan out. Answer: There can be much more concentration of energy both from below the earth and above it when a land mass is completely surrounded by water. Water seals or creates a division from other harmful vibrations. Hence the high places are rarer in atmosphere and vibrations as well.

3rd attempt:
486 AD. Confirmed that work on extending this settlement was

Hartland Point: 'Arturus seems to spend some time looking out from the cliff top . . .'

being carried out around this time, together with fortifications, such as a stockade, and I saw huge wooden gates. Ditches surrounding the whole were widened and made very deep. The side leading up to the settlement was set with large smooth stones so that scaling the sides was made extremely difficult.

It would seem that a dangerous time for this tribe or tribes was coming. Sorry about this, but Arthur was playing a very effective role in getting this work carried out! He took a lot of men from here, so it is logical that those who were left should be well-protected, especially as he has — or feels as if he has — family ties with people here.

He may have returned to the area several times, but I definitely get the date of 502 AD when an attack by sea occurred. The lead-up to this was Arthur leaning against a huge standing stone with his back to it. I could feel a current of power pass down my spine. He projected his mind and 'saw' a number of boats travelling way out at sea yet following the line of the Cornish coast. He knew when their arrival would be.

The next scene — and this is so like a film sequence that I hesitate to tell it — is Arthur with a band of men down on the beach — very stony — concealed in a cave and watching the arrival of about six to eight smallish boats grounding on the shingle. It is dark, or rather more twilight so the invaders can be seen. We attack, taking them completely by surprise and killing the whole of this advance party. There are bodies lying in the water, and I am looking over them and come to one who has a large metal brooch on the front of his jerkin. I lean down to take it off, and then Barney counted us down back to full consciousness! How exciting. Unless I go back I will never know what it was or whether I took it.

Strange Characters

From strange shapes — and places — in Devon to strange characters in the county, and Devon has had her share of these too.

Sabine Baring-Gould wrote a book entitled *Devonshire Characters and Strange Events*. He was the right man to put together such a volume, for he became a legend in his own lifetime. An enigma, he was a man of several parts: squire and parson, the author of books and hymns, including *Onward Christian Soldiers*, he was an enthusiastic explorer of Dartmoor and one of the pioneers in recording the vanishing folk-songs of the Westcountry. Baring-Gould was a larger than life figure: a builder and a landlord, an antiquarian and story-teller, he packed a great deal into his ninety years. He was born in 1834 and died in 1924, but he lives on in his books and hymns.

Some people and some places are inseparable — and here is such a case: you cannot come to Lew Trenchard, either the house or the church, and not be aware of Baring-Gould. You cannot read or refer to the great man and ignore the house and the church. All three are linked in some Holy, human, housing Trinity.

There is a particular magic about Lew Trenchard and here is Baring-Gould describing the house and the grounds as if he were talking to us — or writing a letter.

'From the east wall of the library, a wall extended, ending in what looked like an exceptionally large dovecote. It had one room, approached by steps, furnished as a bedroom and called "The Prophet's Chamber". The wall is pierced by a Gothic Arch and beyond is seen a long avenue of trees, known as "Madam's Walk". Add to this setting the herbaceous borders full of flowers, a granite fountain, always playing, with the figure of an Alsatian gooseherd, imagine it on a sunlit evening.' Describing his library window where he stood at his tall writing desk, he called it 'the glory of the place.

Only one who, like myself, has the happiness to occupy a room with a six-light window, 12 feet wide and 5 feet high, through which the sun pours in and floods the whole room, while without, the keen March wind is cutting, can tell the exhilarating effect it has on the spirit, how it lets the sun in not only through the room, and on one's book or paper, but into the very heart and soul as well.'

Bickford H. C. Dickinson, his grandson, in his biography *Sabine Baring-Gould*, had this to say: 'Among his fellow clergy he was as out of place as an eagle among barn-door fowls, and he seldom troubled to attend either chapter meetings or any of those social and pious gatherings which can so easily occupy a large part of a parson's time . . . In Lew Trenchard itself he is scarcely remembered for any of the things for which he was famous during his lifetime. Rather he is the man who caught boys robbing his orchard and, after reprimanding them, had a basket of eating apples placed regularly at his back door so that they should never again be tempted to steal. He is the parson who each autumn visited every house in the parish to leave a gift of bulbs, calling again without fail the following spring to see them in bloom. He is the man who drove the twenty miles to Okehampton and back in his open dog-cart to give a birthday present of sweets to an ex-choirboy who was at school there; the man who distributed a present of coal each Christmas to every cottage on his estate. There are still those who love to recount stories of his personal kindness, his peculiarities, and his periodic outbursts of impatience, for he was always in a hurry and loathed to be kept waiting by anyone, whether parishioner or visiting bishop. "Usually I absolutely loved him," said one who remembered him very well indeed, "but there were times when I hated him." This remark, from someone who knew him intimately, confirms him as one of those people who can be loved, admired or even detested, according to one's nature and outlook, but who cannot be ignored.'

If for no other reason, Baring-Gould deserves inclusion in 'strange characters' on the strength of his extraordinary courtship and marriage. He was the eldest son of a 'county' family, and when he met his wife-to-be, Grace Taylor, she was a mill-girl of sixteen. Her

Sabine Baring-Gould ' . . . a man of several parts: squire and parson, the author of books and hymns . . . a larger than life figure . . .'▶

'. . . you cannot come to Lew Trenchard, either the house or the church, and not be aware of Baring-Gould.'

parents were poor and, having started work at the age of ten, she was barely literate. The chemistry that brought together two such contrasting characters will remain a romantic mystery. Nobody, for example, will ever know how they first met. At the minister's night-school or when he visited the girl's ill mother? We can only guess about the curate and the Yorkshire girl in their Northcountry romance.

When Baring-Gould wrote his first novel *Through Flood and Flame,* he told the tale of a strange love: a clergyman's son for a poor mill-maid. We can fairly assume that here he was drawing on personal memory rather than a novelist's imagination. In the novel the young man sends his lover to a relative to be educated, and in reality, Baring-Gould did precisely that, sending Grace Taylor to a relation for this very purpose.

She may have been beautiful but they lived in worlds apart, and he was a man almost double her age. We can only guess about the opposition and the gossip. Social divisions were sharply defined in the 1860s and the fact that no member of either family was present at the wedding tells its own hostile story. Despite the enormous gaps in terms of age and social barriers, Grace eventually became

the dignified Lady of the Manor — she was only eighteen when they married. Though not overshadowed by her formidable sophisticated partner, it's fair to say she did not play a large role in the social life of Devon — hardly surprising as she spent the greater part of her married life expecting a child or recovering from confinement. She produced as many as fifteen children — ten daughters and five sons — and in all Grace and Sabine Baring-Gould had 29 grandchildren.

Visitors to Lew Trenchard, in its days as an hotel, were often told of Baring-Gould's inability to recognise his own grandchildren at a party in the lovely old house. But in his defence, Lew House, in pre-electricity days, must have been a dark place, and his eyesight was bad. He had ruined it on a sea voyage, struggling to read by a flickering lantern. In later life, minus his spectacles, he became helpless and almost 'blind'. As a result, he sometimes carried as many as three pairs of spectacles and, on occasions, he would be seen wearing all three perched high on his forehead, having forgotten their whereabouts!

Only some facets in the long eccentric life of a great Devon character — a man surely worthy of his place inside these strange pages.

To move from Baring-Gould to our next character is to move from a study in eccentricity to another in sheer roguery.

Of all the characters who march through the pages of Devon history Bampfylde-Moore Carew must surely be the strangest. Moreover he was responsible for a very odd volume entitled *An Apology for the Life of Mr Bampfylde-Moore Carew.* This autobiography is an excellent example of early 'ghosting' for the 'author' dictated his adventures to a literary friend who gave the tales their bookish shape, padding out his sentences with reflections from Shakespeare and Horace.

From boyhood Bampfylde-Moore Carew became an outcast — but no outcast because society shunned him — he simply rejected respectable society and became 'King of the Beggars'. He could also have been called 'Count Confidence Trickster' or 'Prince of the Imposters', for he was all these. No greater rogue strode across the Devon landscape. He was born at Bickleigh, near Tiverton, in 1693, son of the local Rector, and died fifty-five years later. His bones rest at Bickleigh but in those fifty-five years he travelled far, and his ghost must haunt many places.

As a boy he attended Tiverton School. If his 'autobiography' is to be believed he showed great promise. 'During the first four years of his continuance at Tiverton School, his close application to and delight in his studies gave his friends great hopes that he might one day make a good figure in that honourable profession which his father became so well, and for which he was designed.

'He attained, for his age a very considerable knowledge of the Latin and Greek tongues; but, soon a new exercise or accomplishment engaged all his attentions; this was that of hunting, in which our hero soon made a surprising progress; for besides that agility of limb and courage requisite for leaping over five-barred gates, &c. our hero, by indefatigable study and application, added to it a remarkable cheering halloo to the dogs, of very great service to the exercise, and which we believe was peculiar to himself; and, besides this found out a secret, hitherto known but to himself, of enticing any dog whatever to follow him.'

Dogs — or more precisely hounds — were however responsible for his scholastic career ending at Tiverton. He and some fellow pupils kept a pack of hounds, and one stag hunt caused so much damage to crops that the farmer complained bitterly to the Headmaster and Carew ran away rather than face a severe caning. He then joined a group of gypsies — and so in a way his education of 'Life' began.

In the space available, only a brief profile is possible. But here are just *some* of his incredible exploits. He travelled to Sweden where he collected money, posing as a Presbyterian Minister. He went to Paris, posing this time as a refugee Romanist from Britain. He pretended to be an heroic soldier, wounded at Fontenoy, proudly exhibiting a raw beefsteak attached to his knee: 'my open wound'.

The tragedy is that had he channelled his undoubted talents in other directions he could easily have succeeded as say a soldier or a politician — or a novelist, for his disguises were brilliantly inventive. But, in fact, his only professed profession was a catcher of vermin.

His conduct knew no conscience, especially outrageous being the occasion when he journeyed from Dartmouth to Newcastle by sea. A coal ship in those days was not the most romantic mode of travel, but on such a vessel Bampfylde-Moore Carew fell in love with a doctor's daughter, a Miss Gray. Pretending to be the ship's mate, he swept the young lady off her feet. Her father opposed the relationship, but Carew persuaded her to elope with him, after which he confessed to her that his only occupation was a hunter of vermin. Incredibly she went through with a marriage in fashionable Bath, where they lived in great style for a few weeks until his money was gone, and he was forced to return to his fraudulent ways. The penniless couple then moved to Porchester where an uncle of Carew's, a clergyman, resolved to reform his nephew, promising to find him some suitable employment 'befitting his birth'. The idea of regular work, however, did not appeal to Carew. Instead he carefully studied his uncle's speech and manner, and, one day, left the house, taking with him cassock, gown and bands, setting himself up as a clergyman who had fallen on hard times — a cunning piece of strategy that earned him a good supply of sympathy — and cash.

Sally Jones has concisely pinned to paper some of his cunning tactics.

'Sometimes he posed as a shipwrecked sailor and took advantage of people's generosity; sometimes he claimed his house had burnt down; sometimes he capered round in a blanket pretending to be an escaped lunatic. He also kept a watchful eye on the papers for disasters and as soon as he heard of one he would claim to have lost everything in it and apply for relief. He backed up his story with forged letters, supposedly from magistrates and clergymen. He certainly worked at his 'trade', making a voyage to Newfoundland simply to pass himself off more convincingly as a shipwrecked sailor with detailed knowledge of the places, merchants and agents there. This dedication paid off, for although he'd made a lot of money before, it was nothing compared to what he could now command.'

Anyway his roguery was such that his stock rose high among all the gypsies and tramps in the land, and when their leader Claude Patch passed away, Carew was elected as his successor. He was made King of the Beggars at a great gathering in London, but, in due course, was arrested and tried here in Devon at the Exeter Quarter-Sessions — and was inevitably sentenced and transported to Maryland. He was sold to a planter as a slave — soon he was wearing the iron collar of slavery — for most men it would have been the end of the road. But Carew escaped almost at once and joined a

Bampfylde-Moore Carew: 'No greater rogue strode across the Devon landscape.'▶

group of Indians whom he persuaded to relieve him of his collar. In repayment of this generous act he stole a canoe from them and after a series of adventures got back to London.

As he neared the British shores, though, one fear grew in Carew's mind: the possibility of being 'press ganged' into the Navy. Once more showing brilliant inventiveness, he pricked his arms and chest with a needle and rubbed gun powder and bay salt into his 'wounds' to give the impression that he was a smallpox victim.

Safely back in Britain, he resumed his life of crime and cunning.

According to Sabine Baring-Gould — Carew deservedly got a chapter in his *Devonshire Characters & Strange Events* — 'He died in obscurity . . . It is not known what became of his daughter, the only child he had.'

But according to Carew's literary colleague 'Our hero returned home to the place of his nativity . . . he retired to the west country where he purchased a neat cottage, which he embellished in a handsome style, and lived in a manner becoming a good old English gentleman, respected by his neighbours, and beloved by the poor, to whom his doors were ever open. Here he died full of years and honours, regretted by all.'

And herein lies the fascination of this rascal, disentangling the fact from fiction. His story-teller claims his disguises were endless. Well, if all those recollections are true, then he would have needed several lifetimes, for it's hard to believe that a man could have packed so much into so short a span.

Our third strange character — almost a Mafia-type figure — was the Reverend John Froude. The interesting common denominator in all three is the Church.

John Froude was a contemporary and neighbour of yet another eccentric hunting parson, Jack Russell, and both men appeared to take a keener interest in the pursuit of field sports than in the care of their flocks. A 'reverend gentleman' was apparently more of a leisurely pursuit than an occupation in the nineteenth century.

But whereas Parson Russell's reputation was good, John Froude's was nothing but evil. A graduate from Oxford, he took over the living of Knowstone and Molland from his father in September, 1803. For the next 49 years until his death in 1852 John

Froude held sway over these two remote parishes on the fringe of Exmoor. His methods were vicious and vindictive, enforced by a gang of ruffians who lived at the Rectory, employed by Froude as labourers and kennelmen for his hounds.

In those days landowners still paid tithes, a form of tax, to the Church and should any farmer be behind with his payments, Froude had only to mention what a shame it would be if the errant farmer's hay rick should burn down, or his stock be turned loose, or some mishap occur to his horse or cart, and sure enough that misfortune would overtake the farmer.

His prowess in the hunting field and his open-handed generosity seem to have ensured him a certain popularity and immunity from justice with his sporting neighbours. It was said he could hunt the parish from the top of his church tower and his 'view halloo' could be heard for miles, recalling his hounds at speed.

His activities seem to have stopped short of the criminal and greed does not appear to have been a motive. But John Froude could not bear to be crossed and seems to have taken great pleasure in humiliating other people. The first trait is illustrated by an incident that occurred after he was outbid at auction for a horse. Seeing the animal left by its new owner in a stable some weeks later, Froude managed to place a hemp seed in the poor creature's eye. The horse, nearly driven mad with pain, threw his owner on the ride home.

The chairman of the local magistrates, Mr Karslake, must have upset Froude considerably for he went to great lengths to humiliate him. On being told that a young girl was missing, leaving a shoe and a bloodstained bonnet by the roadside, Karslake organised a search spending much of his own time and money. About ten days later, Froude walked into the crowded courtroom with a little girl by the hand, and asked if this was the maid Karslake had been looking for. She had been kept out of sight at the Rectory with the connivance of her parents, and poor Mr Karslake's pride must have taken a terrible blow from the mirth that greeted Froude's announcement. Times change — no-one would laugh at such a story today.

Despite frequent reports in the press concerning his activities and neglect of his duties, not even the Bishop of Exeter could bring him to heel. Froude refused even to visit the Bishop at South Moulton, saying he was indisposed, and hastily taking to his bed when he heard the Bishop was on his way to Knowstone. But he apparently got nowhere, his remonstrances being greeted with offers of refreshment, flippant replies and the hopes that the Bishop would not catch the mysterious infection.

Against Froude's wishes, a curate was sent to assist him in the running of the parishes, and the poor young man must have led a miserable existence. On one occasion over Sunday lunch Froude, using a favourite trick of his, produced his home-brewed ale, a drink mild in flavour but very potent. When the curate was drunk, Froude suggested to his guests that they venture into his barn and guess the weight of a newly killed pig hung up from a beam. After some ribaldry, Froude said he reckoned the pig weighed about the same as his curate, who was on the fat side. To prove his point, the luckless curate was bundled into a sack and hung from the beam as a counterbalance to the pig — and left there until he sobered up. The congregation went without evensong that day as Froude said he would not take the service and the curate could not.

The one redeeming story in a life full of cruel and malicious incidents was that of his marriage to Miss Halse, which took place late in life. The lady's brothers objected to the insolent attentions Froude had been paying her and lured him to their home. Treating him as he had treated many others, they got him drunk and persuaded him to sign a document saying he would marry Miss Halse, or pay them £20,000. Presumably the brothers had hoped for the money, but to everyone's surprise, Froude decided on matrimony. The match turned out better than anyone expected, his widow referring to Froude as her dear, departed saint — a sentiment with which few people would have agreed.

Salcombe Mystery

Salcombe is not a strange place.

It is, in fact, almost too pretty to be true. Sheltering within the estuary on the South Devon coast, it is a haven for sailors and fishermen. An immediate impression might be that nothing terrible could happen in such an idyllic setting.

But Salcombe is linked to a mystery, baffling and sinister.

Can a woman and her two children just walk out of Life? It seemingly happened here in the spring of 1975. Patricia Allen, an attractive well-dressed woman, and her two children, Victoria, then aged six, and Jonathan, aged seven, form a triangle of dark mystery — something that might have been lifted from the pages of an Agatha Christie novel.

But the question is did they simply walk out of their Devon lives? Or were they murdered? The Police file remains open, but the disappearance of Patricia Allen and her two children could linger on as one of those stories without an ending. Suicide is an impossible prospect—well, almost impossible. Who would have disposed of not one but three bodies in such an act of triple suicide? How could it have been done? And, in any case, everybody agrees on one thing: Patricia Allen was a devoted mother. Suicide then is a non-starter.

Did Patricia Allen plan to walk out—for a second time—on a husband? She did it once before. But then she was traced. This time, though, there is not a suggestion or clue as to her whereabouts—or those of her children.

It is as if they have quite simply vanished into thin air.

What kind of woman was Patricia Allen?

Photographs portray a stylish dresser and a woman who liked soaking up the sun. Her love life was chequered. In 1956 she married, but walked out on her husband within twelve months. She then made friends with an American serviceman and spent some months in Canada and the United States in 1966 and 1967. Back in Britain she met Anthony John Allen, then known as Anthony John Angel. They married in 1968.

But when Mr Allen was away from home, in a period from March 1972 to April 1973, Mrs Allen became friendly with different men in Huntingdonshire and Leicestershire. However, the family came together again in April 1973.

It was not until the following year that the Allens came to the Westcountry. In September they were at a caravan site at Dawlish; in November they were living in Ashelton Road, Torquay, and soon afterwards Mr Allen went to work at the Marine Hotel in Salcombe, and Patricia Allen moved to her last known address: a flat at Powderham Villa, Devon Road, Salcombe.

The plain basic facts are these: Patricia Allen left that Salcombe flat on 26 May 1975 and was never seen again by anyone except her husband.

Forty-eight hours later, Mr Allen told the Police, she returned to the flat in Devon Road, collected the two children—and disappeared. Mr Allen however did not report them missing. He believed that she 'had gone off with a boyfriend', and, as a result, the Police did not begin enquiries until four months later.

Precisely what Mr Allen told the Police has never been disclosed. But the Police later made a statement saying that he had given 'many versions' of the events—and all of them had been checked out thoroughly.

There are elements in this case which prove fact *can* be stranger than fiction. For example, only the concern and curiosity of a cousin brought the Police on to the scene. 'This cousin was the sole member of her family with whom Mrs Allen had a close relationship,' Detective Chief Superintendent Bissett told us. John Bissett, who was born at Okehampton, is today the Head of Devon and Cornwall CID, the man who has been largely responsible for the intensive Police activity in the search for Mrs Allen and her children. 'Not until the cousin had returned from his Devon holiday did he, in fact, report his concern about Mrs Allen's disappearance. He wasn't satisfied with the story that she had gone off with someone else. So we were four months late in starting our enquiries. There may have been rumours circulating in and around Salcombe but nobody reported the matter.

'Mr Allen said his wife returned two days later—on the evening of

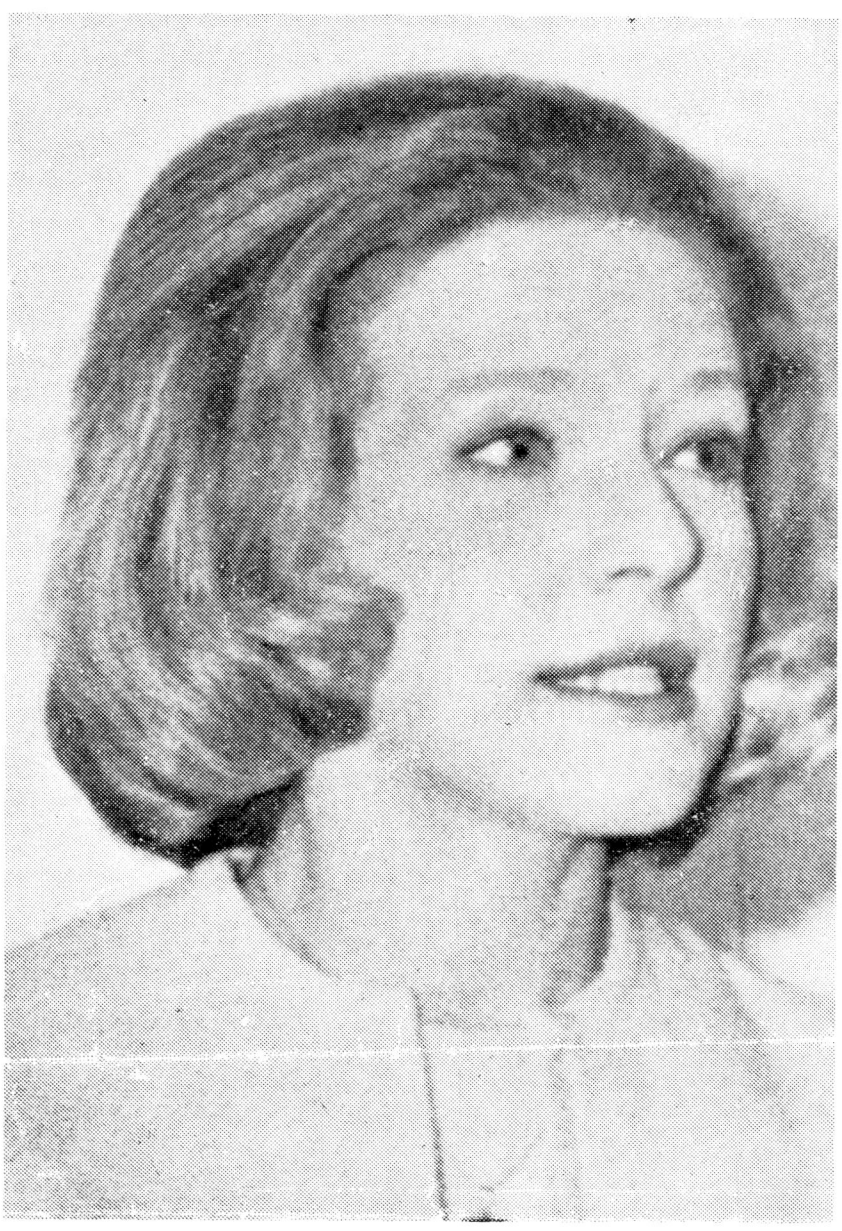

Patricia Allen: '. . . it is now unlikely that the extraordinary disappearance of this attractive forty-year-old woman and her two children will ever be solved.'

Patricia Allen's 'last known address: a flat at Powderham Villa, Devon Road, Salcombe.'

28 May—to collect the children, and drove off to Totnes railway station. The three of them have not been seen since. We checked the station there . . . but nothing.

'Once alerted, we put on a massive operation, an international operation because Interpol were involved . . . government departments, local authorities, passport offices, foreign embassies, friends and relations, and mere aquaintances. Our enquiries have stretched throughout this country and abroad. We have had dozens of reported "sightings" in this country, and about a dozen overseas . . . we've checked them all out . . . but have still drawn a blank.'

Following his wife's disappearance in May 1975 Mr Allen lost his job at the Marine Hotel in Salcombe. He then became employed by Mrs Eunice Yabsley, a widow who was running the Galley Restaurant, also in Salcombe. Shortly after his wife vanished, Mr Allen set up home with Mrs Yabsley. The couple eventually left

Devon and now live in the London area.

Police did finally locate Patricia Allen's Volkswagen at Shadycombe, a car parking area, near Salcombe, by the estuary. Astonishingly it had remained there unmentioned and undetected for as long as four months. What was never discovered, though, was the family's small rowing dinghy which went missing at this time.

Throughout the autumn and winter of 1975 a massive Police search was in operation. For the first time in a British hunt, the Police used a remarkably sophisticated camera, mounted on an autogyro, which can tell experts where animal matter has blended with the soil. Divers searched the harbour at Salcombe and neighbouring creeks. Dogs, especially trained to locate human remains, were brought down to Devon to help in the search—the same dogs who had been sent out of Britain, loaned to the United Nations, to find the bodies of Israeli soldiers in the desert during the war between Israel and Egypt in the Sinai Desert. It was a hunt only surpassed by the Genette Tate investigations in more recent times.

Yet the riddle remained: not a strand of evidence.

Though the Police had alerted every airport, sea terminal, bus station and railway station in Britain, a wall of baffling mystery continued.

When Patricia Allen left her flat in Salcombe, she left a full wardrobe of brand new clothes for herself and the children. Since then she has made no claim for social security, and there have been no applications for school places for the children. Moreover their health registration documents have remained unchanged. Even money owed to Patricia Allen has not been claimed.

It all does seem to add up as if this 5 foot 4 inches tall woman with a slight Northcountry accent and dyed blonde neck-length hair had become invisible, taking with her two children, to whom she was devoted.

'If the children were at school somewhere else,' said a thoughtful John Bissett, 'their surname may have been changed but it's highly unlikely that children of their age would have assumed different christian names and it would be *very* difficult for them to have got away with assumed names for any length of time.'

Precisely one year after their disappearance, John Bissett made this statement through the press: 'Our concern is for the welfare of the children and their mother. There may be a rational explanation for their disappearance and Mrs Allen may be living a normal life somewhere. If so, we urgently appeal to her to contact us. We have no wish to become involved in a domestic situation but we cannot leave this mystery unsolved.'

Incredibly though, more than five years on, it remains precisely that.

'Do you think that Patricia Allen went somewhere else—overseas perhaps—to start a new life with a new partner?' we asked.

'Naturally I must keep an open mind,' reflected John Bissett, 'but I am very, very doubtful. We followed up leads that took us to Gibraltar, Germany and Holland, but they have all failed to lead us to either Mrs Allen or to her body.'

'That then brings you to the conclusion that all three of them are dead. What makes you come to that conclusion?'

John Bissett looked very serious.

'My firm belief is that all three are dead. I just don't believe that a mother and her two children can completely disappear. If Mrs Allen and her two children were alive and elsewhere—say Canada or the United States, which has been suggested—then I am quite satisfied through the efforts of Interpol we should have found them. It may be possible for one person to disappear, but here we're talking about a family of three, and two of them small children.

'I've seen what was left behind. There were children's toys, their favourite clothes . . . pictures, very personal possessions . . . not the sort of thing people would leave behind if they were planning to make another start elsewhere . . . something very bad happened to Mrs Allen and those two children. But the file remains open. We've not had any developments now for about twelve months but I—and the Police Force—will never forget them.'

Never is a big word.

But you get the impression it is now unlikely the extraordinary disappearance of this attractive forty-year-old woman and her two children will ever be solved.

A sinister story then—and one without any kind of real ending.

'It must have been a terrible experience to live through that night . . .' ▶

Lynmouth — A North Devon Disaster

A phenomenon occurring once only with such cataclysmic results on human life and property that it was deemed a National Disaster is surely entitled to be called a strange happening.

Such was the flood disaster that struck the picturesque North Devon coastal village of Lynmouth on the night of 15/16 August 1952. At least 34 people were killed or missing, 42 houses were totally destroyed, 72 were ruined beyond repair and a further 20 were seriously damaged. Over 100 vehicles were swept out to sea, many of them twisted and crushed beyond recognition. Over Exmoor as a whole countless bridges were swept away, hundreds of homes flooded and miles of road ripped up.

The phenomenon was the rain — it was estimated that between mid-morning on the 15th and 9 a.m. on the 16th, nine inches of rain fell; a total only twice equalled since records have been kept and more than three months' normal fall.

A study of the map makes it all too clear why disaster hit Lynmouth that night. The river system of the northern part of Exmoor, that wild, desolate upland area of peat and bog, drains towards the North Devon coast. Because of the hard sandstone hog's back cliffs between Porlock and Foreland Point, the streams are forced along the coast in a westerly direction until the entire system finds access to the sea at Lynmouth, falling 1,500 feet in four miles. The East Lyn River is fed by eight main tributaries and countless smaller ones, and the West Lyn by four main streams, all converging on Lynmouth where the two rivers join within a quarter of a mile of the sea.

Exmoor usually acts as a sponge, but The Chains, the most

'. . . rescue forces from all over the country mobilised.'

impermeable area of Exmoor immediately behind Lynmouth, were already saturated by continuous rainfall during one of the wettest and most miserable of Augusts. The final straw was a cloudburst over The Chains that evening from a sky described as dark, lowering, purple. It was calculated that five inches fell in one hour.

All over Exmoor the streams rose with frightening rapidity. Trickles became streams, streams became rushing rivers, and the rivers raging torrents of destruction. And all that water had only one outlet — Lynmouth.

This was no gradual build-up of water with time to issue flood warnings, but a deluge terrifying in its intensity and suddenness. A Police Constable was literally knocked off his motorbike by a sheet of water and when he returned to the hotel at Exford to warn the surrounding villages, within four minutes the water was up to his chest. No warnings were issued to Barbrook and Lynmouth. There was no time.

'The devastation was beyond belief . . .'

Those same rocky banks and boulder-strewn river beds admired by visitors became a death trap. Caught in their steeply falling canyons the raging waters demolished everything in their path — trees, bridges, cottages, boulders of enormous size — all were swept onwards before the great force of water.

The tragedy was summed up by *The North Devon Journal-Herald:* 'Lynmouth, that little village on the beautiful boulder-strewn River Lyn — which inspired some of the classics of British literature and drew thousands from all over the world to admire its simple charm, is no more. In a few, terrifying hours the crystal whispering river that contributed so much to its sheer beauty, destroyed it.'

It must have been a terrible experience to live through that night. All over Exmoor and in Lynmouth in particular there were many valiant deeds, many courageous rescues and there must be many unsung heroes and unrecorded acts of bravery. But for many, marooned in their homes, surrounded by boiling angry waters, there was no hope and no help.

At Lynmouth the Lyndale Hotel bore the brunt of the onslaught. The hotel became a virtual island when the West Lyn River changed its course, because the choked Lyndale Bridge was acting as a dam. A mound of debris over thirty feet high piled up against the hotel and may well have saved the building, forming a protecting barrier against the pounding of the waters.

Inside were forty guests and staff, who floor by floor moved higher up the building as the floodwaters rose. For them it must have been the most terrifying night of their lives, huddled together in total darkness, for the electricity had long since gone, as all around the waters roared and swirled and huge boulders battered at their refuge. Destruction must have seemed inevitable. What must it have been like for those who endured the long hours alone — and for those who did not survive?

The devastation was beyond belief. Whole buildings washed away, gaping holes in those remaining, sagging floors and roofs, household possessions and debris everywhere. The only road down to Lynmouth ended in a desolation of boulders, tree trunks and rubble that formed the new course gouged out for itself by the West Lyn River. The bed of the East Lyn was six feet higher than formerly because of the quantity of boulders. The sea was discoloured for a mile or more and the whole bay was littered with trees, telegraph poles, twisted cars and bloated carcases of animals.

'. . . the whole bay was littered with trees, telegraph poles, twisted cars and bloated carcases of animals.'

As the enormity of the disaster became known, rescue forces from all over the country mobilised. The whole village was evacuated to Lynton, not only for their safety — only a few inches of rainfall could bring the boulders and debris choking the rivers higher up crashing down on the stricken village — but also to enable the rescue work to proceed unhindered. Within hours the County Council had gathered together over 100 workmen and Police, firemen, Civil Defence and a host of volunteers had begun work. Their first grim task was to search for the bodies of the dead. Work was hindered in the early days because many of the roads leading to Lynmouth had been rendered impassable by the floods and the area was cordoned off to stop sightseers.

But the salvage of Lynmouth was a Herculean task and without the help of the Army and their 'heavy equipment' it could well have been abandoned — left a shambolic ruin. They came with cranes and bulldozers, mobile generators and excavators and with all their technical know-how and stoic good humour. It took an hour for each piece of heavy equipment, held by a Scammel recovery vehicle, to grind down the battered hill to Lynmouth. Work went on day and night. The noise from the power saws, gelignite, bulldozers and excavators, was deafening, but within five days miraculously the initial stage of emergency clearance was completed. The sea wall had been temporarily repaired and two Bailey bridges connected Lynmouth once more with the outside world. But it was not until 14 September that Lynmouth people were allowed back to their homes and some semblance of life returned to the little village.

Lynmouth today is an attractive holiday resort, and to those who have forgotten the disaster, few scars remain. But for many, much of its former charm has been lost. In the wake of the flood an official report was prepared. To prevent a recurrence of such a tragedy, and so that Lynmouth should be seen to be safe, it was recommended that the river channels be widened and stabilised, and that no buildings should remain on the area around the confluence of the East and West Lyn. The Lyndale Hotel that had survived so bravely, and its neighbour, the Lyn Valley Hotel, were demolished, leaving a wide open space in the heart of the village. The East Lyn flows between man-made banks and summer visitors looking down on the diminished trickle of water, almost lost in its great wide channel, must find it very hard to believe once upon an August night it was capable of such destruction.

A Kindred Spirit

On this journey across Devon we have been reminded of the fact that one thing leads to another—and that personal contact is important in any quest. Take, for example, Sally Dodd of *The Tavistock Times*. Hearing of our search for the strange and the unusual, Sally said 'Contact Michael Wreford . . . you'll have a lot in common.' And how right she was, for in Plymouth-born Michael Wreford we met a kindred spirit: someone who loves delving into Devon's past, a man with a special interest in the off-beat and the unusual.

Here then are some of the fascinating stories he told us at his home in Okehampton. He works for the South Western Electricity Board at Chagford on the edge of Dartmoor and is a freelance writer in his off-duty hours.

'I'm Devon born and bred,' Michael Wreford explained, 'but I'm not the Sir Francis Drake kind of Devonian. I love inland Devon.' Naturally enough then Dartmoor draws him like a magnet, and his first story concerns arguably the greatest Englishman of them all and grim Dartmoor Prison at Princetown. Standing over 1,400 feet above sea level, and set in this great Devon wilderness, the Prison—even today—has a forbidding and forbidden air.

A certain David Davies had been apprehended and charged at Shrewsbury for stealing two shillings. The sentence was more than severe—three years penal servitude plus ten years Preventative Detention, and this at the age of 67.

Davies seemed to enjoy some of his time at Dartmoor and worked with the animals on the farms. His particular knack was with sheep, where he almost seemed to talk to them. Furthermore, he gave the sheep names and they responded to them.

However, in 1911, help was at hand in the redoubtable form of the then Mr Winston Churchill who was Home Secretary. He was per-

The young Mr Winston Churchill; Home Secretary when Davies was in Dartmoor Prison (far left): 'A prison ought not to be looked upon as a Home of Refuge . . .'

sonally looking into the schedule of habitual prisoners, and he came across the entry relating to Davies. He noted the ridiculous contrast between the crime and the punishment, and he called for a comprehensive report. This showed that the gentle Davies relished his reputation as a friend of the sheep, and also the huge sentences he had received, totalling 58 years of which he had served 38 years.

His behaviour in prison was impeccable, very docile—a model prisoner in fact. The punishments were worse than the crime he had committed; and perhaps he was happy to serve the sentences because he had only one known relative in the world — in Texas.

Mr Churchill, never one to mince his words, promptly issued an official Communiqué aptly named 'The Old Shepherd of Dartmoor'. He visited Dartmoor and was able to confirm all the findings of the report and this enabled him to release Davies on licence.

'A prison ought not to be looked upon as a Home of Refuge; a cloistered seclusion, where aged sinners may placidly, contentedly, healthfully and happily watch the sunset of life.'

Davies was subsequently released and was taken to a farm in Wales, where no doubt his expertise with sheep was put to good use—even if the accents were different!

★ ★ ★ ★ ★

Here too, thought Michael Wreford, is a tale worth telling about Wonson Manor at Throwleigh. The Manor, for many years, was occupied by the well-known Northmore family, several of whom were Members of Parliament. The most celebrated was William Northmore the younger, born in 1690 and probably the richest member of the family. He did, however, lead a full and somewhat hectic life. He was amongst other things MP for Okehampton, as well as Mayor, Churchwarden and Recorder of the town. His domestic duties were erratic, and he married three times, but none of his wives produced any children. He was popular and kind hearted, but like many people of his time he gambled heavily, often to the extreme. In fact, on one evening he lost as much as £17,000 on the turn of one card, the Ace of Diamonds. After that expensive experience, he had a replica of the card painted on the wood panelling of a room at the Manor where it is to this day. The story goes that every night William Northmore would—and still probably does—shake his fist at the card and curse it instead of saying his prayers!

Dartmoor Prison 'even today has a forbidding and forbidden air.'

For his next adventure into the strange and unusual of Devon, Michael Wreford came back to his home town of Okehampton.

> Behind the Chantry mute be read
> The initial scroll of the burgher dead
> Stout of heart, they esteem the wight
> Who reads the letters at dead of night
> Though the moon be glinted back the white
> From the Oriel lights of the chantry aisle
> Never pass but breathe a prayer
> For the souls best peace of Master Gayer

These lines refer to Benjamin Gayer sometimes known as 'Benjie Geare'. This former Okehampton worthy was one of the most famous of Dartmoor characters. 'Benjie' seems to have been a very respected Okehampton businessman, very philanthropic and a pillar of the Church.

His business as a wool merchant flourished, and this occupied much of his time; but he was very interested in the civic affairs of the town and he was Mayor of Okehampton on five occasions.

One story about him which has been passed down the centuries, is that during his last term of office as Mayor, several of the Okehampton merchants lost their ships to the Portuguese pirates and as a result, he, as Mayor, started a fund for these distressed people. Whilst he was accumulating this money his own ship was pillaged and as a result he diverted the money to his own use.

It can definitely be established that he lived in the property now occupied by Cecil Cole Ltd, Ironmonger of Okehampton. This was then his town house in Okehampton and the letters 'BG' were erected high on the gable end facing Fore Street. Today, these same letters are on the building but not in the same position.

Harold Wright, that most popular figure who traded as James Wright, told Michael Wreford some twenty years ago how the letters came to be altered. It seems that at the turn of the last century Harold's father, James Wright, carried out some major work on the premises, and during the repairs the letters were removed and there was no intention of replacing them at that time. James Wright was warned that 'Evil' would befall him if the letters were omitted and although he scoffed at this, trouble was in store. First a workman fell from near the top of the house, being seriously injured, and almost immediately there was a fire on the premises.

James did not wait for a third misfortune and arranged for the letters to be refixed, but this time at the rear of the property, where they can be seen today, although not easily.

Benjie was married to a woman called Sarah and they lived happily together, although without any children. When he died in 1701 he left his complete estate to his widow, with the simple request that she should pray nightly for the repose of his soul!

Whether she did this I do not know but suffice to say she soon married a Mr Bridges and together they continued to live in the same house. Legend has it that all seemed well at the beginning of the marriage, but alas, Benjie soon seemed to take more than a hand!

The first occurrence was when Mr Bridges was awakened by his new wife in a state of shock, praying and asking the good Lord for protection. Her condition was such that medical aid was sought during the night and she did calm down in the end.

However in the morning she confided in a servant and the exact

Wonson Manor at Throwleigh 'was occupied for many years by the well known Northmore family, several of whom were MPs.'

words are said to be as follows:

'Oh Peggy, Peggy, I am an unhappy woman. He that is dead and gone has appeared to me. I was between sleeping and waking and I felt a cold hand on my cheek, and on opening my eyes I saw Benjamin standing before me with his countenance full of anger.'

It was obvious that Benjie was annoyed at the early marriage, and he continued to haunt not only Sarah, but her friends as well.

To try and lay this ghost, the Okehampton Vicar was contacted and asked for his help. He took the matter very seriously and carefully planned a ceremony with Bell, Book and Candle, and including twelve of his local clerical colleagues.

Benjie actually died at Kigbeare Manor, then known as 'Kegbeare' which he owned as well, and at the time of his death an oil painting hung within the manor. When this property was sold to the Newton family, the painting was taken to Millaton Manor at Bridestowe, where it hung for many years.

In May 1911 one of the largest furniture sales the area has ever seen was held at Millaton and yes, lot 34 was simply catalogued as 'oil painting—Mayor of Okehampton Mr Geare'. What a tragedy of family history lies behind this bald statement. It aroused tremendous interest; and at the two-day sale it was purchased for the then very princely sum of £27 by Mr Nainby Luxmore of that Okehampton family.

★　★　★　★　★

But we thought Michael Wreford's most fascinating story concerned himself—and this time not a shred of legend—in fact a first-hand experience; a reminder too that Devon's strange character and quality do not necessarily live in the distant past. This is what Michael told us:

Little did I realize when I moved to that delightful moorland town of Chagford to work that I would become closely involved with the mystery of 'Mahala', a local ghost.

To start from the beginning; wool has always been part of

◀ 'BG'—letters recalling Benjamin Gayer in
Fore Street, Okehampton, today.

Devon's industry, and Chagford was of some importance with a large Mill at Factory Cross, near Chagford Bridge, which around 1800 employed well over a thousand people. The bell would sound for the start of work and anyone not on time would be left outside the iron gates for half an hour, and one can visualize this on a cold, misty and wet winter morning.

The Manager's house was next to the mill and there were no windows in the house, other than on the wall facing the Mill; of course the tale is that it was so that the manager could watch the mill and the workers all the time.

The Mill finally closed in 1848; the churning of the water wheel stopped and the continual noise of the machinery ceased. The cottages at Factory Cross in front of the disused Mill were still occupied and the glow of the peat and wool fires could be seen in the cold Dartmoor nights.

However, the water from the Teign continued to flow underneath the cottages and, according to folklore, it was here that Mahala Northcott was swept into the river and was drowned in 1867. From then the ghost of that beautiful young girl is said to haunt the site.

As the years went by land and associated buildings were acquired by the early electricity supply pioneers, and after 41 years the leat was again put to good use for, in 1891, the moorland was one of the foremost in the country in receiving a supply of electricity. This site housed the small generating station and still does to this day, although ownership has passed to the Central Electricity Generating Board.

Apart from the former Manager's house, the cottages fell into disrepair, but the stories of Mahala continued throughout the years.

In 1972 I had a surprise visit from a descendant who decided to make a visit to the site of his forebears' cottage. To preserve the anonymity of this man, and in view of the fact that he has since died, I'll call him Bob. He was a man of some professional standing, and well-known in the electronic field.

Bob applied for permission to explore the ruins and discovered that the local manager was an old school friend. This coincidence

'It was here that Mahala Northcott was swept into the river and was drowned in 1867. From then the ghost of that beautiful young girl is said to haunt the site.' ▶

and reunion was of course the key to a conducted tour of the electricity generating equipment behind the normally locked gates. The Mill buildings had of course been demolished and the site overgrown except where in use. The two engineers thoroughly enjoyed their technical discourse and reunion.

Apart from the equipment, Bob's main interest was of course the old Mill Cottage, where his forebears had lived, but alas all that remained was part of one wall and a pile of granite stones. There was no flooring and trees and bushes had taken their place.

Bob was a keen amateur student of geology, and as a memento of his visit he collected a piece of Dartmoor granite, and in due course took it back home with him.

This could have been the end of the story, and the stone could have remained on some dark shelf, forgotten. However, Bob's wife had become interested in the subject and wanted to have the stone psychometrized. Psychometry is the process whereby a medium handles an object and then gives a reading.

Now, we must remember that Bob was a qualified engineer and a practical man, and like all engineers had little regard for anything that could not be proved by hard fact. He decided therefore to disprove the science of psychometry once and for all to his wife. He took the weatherbeaten stone and sent it to a medium.

It was some time later that a reading was received and Bob was astonished and impressed with the accuracy. I have seen the report. Here are extracts which are of particular and accurate relevance.

'Extreme feeling of cold and despair, also grave disappointment . . . the person that has had a throat condition. (Bob had at the time.) I can see a low white building resembling a farmhouse or cottage situated in a valley surrounded by high ground. I sense extreme peace and solitude in this area . . . (this is rather an apt description of the site).

'Once again the feelings of extreme cold and a strong smell of decay and decomposition. I do not like the feelings brought about by this stone. I feel it came from unhappy ground almost a place of sinister happenings. I feel that the owner (of the stone) would not know of this, but on checking it could be discovered that there is death by drowning in this vicinity. I would suggest that this piece of stone is disposed of quickly by placing it near water.

'I hear the name Bob . . . also Matty or Metty. And Jane too. (The last three have no known relevance to Bob, but his Christian name

Author, Rosemary Anne Lauder

was derived).

'I have with me an airman killed during wartime, whilst in the air. He says "I felt no pain . . . it was over in a flash". (This has nothing to do with the mill site but it has considerable personal relevance to Bob who was in the RAF during wartime).

'I still get this "drowning" condition, or even suicidal tendencies. Please get rid of this quickly. (Bob's wife did).'

Bob was impressed and shocked at the amazing accuracy of the reading, and as an engineer, he began to wonder whether there was some technical or rational explanation.

The following year when Bob and his family were once again on holiday on Dartmoor, Bob resolved to further investigate the matter and he had with him a scintillation type of meter; that is an instrument which will detect and register the amount of radiation. Unfortunately he called at a time when his old school friend was away on holiday and he could not obtain access to the site, but, on impulse, took various readings at various points. He was not altogether surprised to find the readings were much higher around the ruins of the cottage and of course where Mahala is said to have lived. The readings also seemed to be higher than normal for the area, although not dangerous I hasten to add. This only whetted Bob's interest and he was determined to continue with his investigations.

It was in the summer of 1975 when he and his family once again came on holiday to Dartmoor. John, the manager, had retired, and I now occupied his desk. An appointment was duly made for access to the site.

I well remember that warm and sunny afternoon as Bob, another electronic engineer, a very learned Professor of Electrical Engineering, myself, and others making a party of eleven drove to the site.

Our object, of course, was to try and find evidence of the presence of the ghost of Mahala, but also to try and establish whether there was any connection between the apparently high gamma ray reading, and the so very accurate psychometry reading.

I had entered the gates of the site on countless occasions, but on that day I became conscious that it seemed cooler as I led the party in. I walked towards the trees covering the ruins of the cottage and it appeared darker than usual. I feel now that I should mention one member of our party. She was, in fact, a rather lively little West Highland terrier, who belonged to the Research Engineer. The terrier refused to go near the site of the cottage. She was happy to run around the rest of the premises, but would stop dead in her tracks at every approach. This dog, normally a very obedient animal, despite all coaxing from her owner and from us all, steadfastly refused to enter.

So far as the gamma ray readings were concerned nothing conclusive was discovered although many theories were bandied about by my learned colleagues, and our discussions went on into early evening.

So, perhaps as we attempt to look into the unknown, we must forget about trying to register the facts on an electronic device. However, I will never forget the feelings brought about by the little West Highland terrier.

Each day as I drive past the site of the old Mill, I still think about that day and I often stop and look around, just hoping to glimpse Mahala, and, do you know, I believe that one day I will.

The Man They Couldn't Hang

Few cases in the annals of crime can be as strange as that of John 'Babbacombe' Lee, who cheated the hangman's noose not once but three times, and has gone down in history as the man they couldn't hang.

Since that day in February 1885, despite much debate and investigation, no satisfactory solution has ever been found as to just how he managed to evade the sentence of death passed on him for the murder of Miss Emma Keyse. History has been so taken up with the macabre ending that events leading up to it have been largely ignored. From start to finish the story is full of unsolved mysteries and unsatisfactory explanations.

John Lee was accused of the particularly brutal murder of his elderly employer. Yet he had no motive, for over the years Miss Keyse had shown him nothing but exceptional kindness and, had he been tried today, it is doubtful whether any jury would have convicted him.

John Lee came from a decent hard-working family at Abbotskerswell. His first job was as 'the boy' at The Glen, Babbacombe, the home of Miss Keyse. Against strong parental opposition he determined on a career in the Navy and eventually he had his way, apparently doing well and winning a progress prize. Then, at the age of eighteen, he was struck down with pneumonia, and invalided out.

Throughout his years at sea Miss Keyse had kept in touch with Lee and now she came to his aid, finding him a post as a footman. Here he made his first mistake — he pawned some of his employer's silver and was caught. Six months hard labour followed, but still

◀ 'John "Babbacombe" Lee who cheated the hangman's noose not once but three times.'

EXTRA SUPPLEMENT to the "DEVON COUNTY STANDARD," January 31st, 1885.

THE BABBACOMBE TRAGEDY.—Views of the Glen (interior and exterior), with Portraits of the Witnesses, Officials, and Prisoner.

PRICE ONE PENNY.

64

Miss Keyse kept faith with Lee. When she could not find him a job anywhere else, she took him on herself, although only temporarily. John Lee was now twenty. During his early life one person had rescued him from, firstly misfortune and, secondly, his own stupidity. Why this elderly, well-connected former lady-in-waiting to Queen Victoria should show such concern for a country lad is another mystery, but John Lee had every reason to be fond of her, and none at all to murder her.

The household at The Glen consisted of Eliza and Jane Neck, two elderly servants of around fifty years standing, and the cook, Lee's step-sister Elizabeth Harris. Although no-one knew at the time, it later became apparent that she was pregnant. On the night of 14 November 1884 events followed their usual pattern except that Elizabeth Harris went to bed early, unwell. John Lee went to sleep on his makeshift bed in the pantry; Eliza and Jane Neck went upstairs, leaving a pot of cocoa on the hob for their mistress, who often stayed up until gone midnight.

Many years after he was released from prison, Lee wrote his own version of the affair, which not surprisingly differed from the evidence given at the trial. He states that he was woken by a shout of 'fire' and went upstairs to look for Miss Keyse, helped by the other servants. Unable to find her he went downstairs and found the dining room so full of smoke he smashed a window to let in some air, and in so doing cut his arm. Lying on the floor, surrounded by smouldering paper, was poor Miss Keyse, her head terribly injured and her throat cut. She had been dragged from the hall where a huge pool of blood marked the spot of the actual murder, only some eight feet nine inches from Lee's bed, and separated from it by a partition wall not reaching to the ceiling. Lee claimed he was a heavy sleeper; the prosecution maintained no-one could have slept through the sound of Miss Keyse's head being hit repeatedly with a hatchet. Jane Neck said that it was she who opened the windows in the dining room and only later was one of them broken. This point was important because Lee helped her downstairs, leaving a bloodstain on her nightgown caused, according to him, from the wound in-

◄ **Supplement to the** *Devon County Standard*, **January, 1885, illustrating the Babbacombe tragedy. Views of 'The Glen' with portraits of witnesses, officials and prisoner.**

curred by smashing the window. Today a simple blood test would have solved the problem; in 1884 it helped to convict him. Lee's step-sister gave evidence of threats she had heard him making against Miss Keyse—who had apparently reduced his wages by six-pence — that he would set fire to the house and watch it burn, and that he would get his revenge on her.

At the trial both the Necks and Elizabeth Harris described how they searched upstairs for Miss Keyse, only going downstairs when the smoke became too dense. Their evidence conflicts with Lee's version as to who found the body first, what state of dress he was in, and who opened the windows and when. Yet one of the witnesses who was called to the house to help put out the fire admitted it was so dark 'he could hardly see what he was doing'.

Could two elderly women, roused from their sleep at five o'clock on a November morning to find their house on fire and their mistress missing, be relied upon to remember events with any accuracy?

The defence did not press either of these points; in fact the defence was almost non-existent and in those days the accused was not allowed into the witness box. The prosecution case rested mainly on the fact that the house had not been broken into and the murderer had, therefore, to be an inmate. The defence, conducted by a barrister who had first offered his services to the other side, could only suggest that as Elizabeth Harris was pregnant, she must have had a lover; she had gone to bed early that day, the first time she had ever done so, and she was the first up to give the alarm.

Not surprisingly, Lee was found guilty and sentenced to death. Again and again in his own version, Lee reiterates that he did not kill Miss Keyes. Had he done so, would he have been stupid enough to hide the oil can, used to start fires in different parts of the house, beside his own bed? Or put the knife, possibly used in the murder, into one of his own drawers? Did he really want two old women whom he had known for many years, and his own step-sister, to perish in the fire? And would he have waited around until he was arrested if he had been guilty of a crime for which he had no motive and which brought him no profit?

Whilst waiting for the sentence to be carried out, Lee was visited by the vicar of Abbotskerswell to whom he made a statement that was considered important enough to be sent to the Home Secretary, Sir William Harcourt. In it Lee 'not altogether exculpated himself from guilt but implicated another person who he alleged was the guilty murderer.' This statement was discredited by Sir William— a friend of Miss Keyse — and has not been mentioned since. Another mystery is why Elizabeth Harris should have testified so vehemently against her step-brother — was she protecting someone else? In a letter to his sister, written shortly before his expected execution, Lee says, 'It must be some very hard hearted persons for to let me die for nothing. All the witnesses will and must appear before our Saviour for what they have said against me and to answer for my life . . . They have not told six words truth that is, the servants and that lovely step-sister who carries her character with her . . . Have you heard from K F or seen them, you know who I mean, Your very affectionate brother who is dead to the world.' K F could mean his fiancée, Kate Farmer, to whom Lee had written in the October saying he was unsettled, tired of service and looking about for something else that she might not like, and was willing to release her from their engagement.

Lee gives a moving account of his own trial. He describes how it felt, worn out after months of prison life, after endless questioning and suspense, after being dragged from one place to another, to finally appear in the dock. If the prisoner was pale and trembled because of the tension and his physical state, he was considered to be suffering from a guilty conscience. If, on the other hand, said Lee, the prisoner betrayed no emotions he was accused of being a heartless villain quite capable of committing the crime.

Lee also describes the dream he is supposed to have had on the eve of his execution, told the following morning to the chaplain and his warders. He says he walked through parts of the jail he had never seen, that he stood on the scaffold and the bolts were drawn, and three times failed to release the trap door. In his account he tells us — surely the only account of what it feels like to be so nearly hanged — of his journey to the gallows, exactly corresponding to his dream. He recalls he didn't think of anything in particular, only disinterested curiosity as to how the gallows worked. He remembers seeing the reporters crowded at the prison windows to watch him die and he remembers a bird hopping about in the prison garden. Then he was bound and pinioned, his head placed in a hood, and he felt the rope harsh against his neck. He refused to confess, maintaining his innocence up to what should have been the end. The order was given, Lee dropped a few inches, and stopped. For what seemed to him like an eternity, and was in fact six minutes, he remained balancing on tiptoe, the rope tight around his neck whilst the warders jumped up and down on the trapdoor. It must have been an experience ghastly beyond the powers of imagination. Eventually he was led away whilst the mechanics were checked, and made to work with no apparent difficulty. Again Lee went through the gruesome motions — bound, pinioned, head in sack, rope round neck, sickening thud of trap being operated and again, a drop of a few inches only. Again jumping up and down by warders and executioner failed to budge the doors. Lee says this time he was just pushed to one side, still with the cap on his head whilst the door was again examined. By this time the warders and executioner were getting desperate; the situation had lost all vestige of dignity and it is difficult to know who was supposed to be the more upset — the prisoner or his jailers.

The third attempt was no more successful but all Lee seems to remember as he was moved off the trap is that he was suffocating because of the hood. When this was removed he says he clearly remembers the terrible state of the warders and chaplain. By the laws of England, the chaplain told him, he could not be put on the scaffold again. His dream had come true.

The explanation at the time was that the boards of the trap were swollen by recent rain, but Lee writes he heard afterwards that the bolts holding the doors were new and whilst opening perfectly when there was no weight above, jammed under pressure. His next recollection was of exercising in the prison garden and seeing a freshly dug grave — his own!

His sentence was commuted to penal servitude for life and he served 22 years before being released. His story gives a horrific insight into the rigours of prison life at the turn of the century but he survived and in 1907 came home to his mother at Abbotskerswell.

There is another possible explanation as to why the trap-doors failed to work. A press cutting, dated March 1945, quotes a letter from a Mr J. R. Pile of 39, Torrington Street, Bideford, saying that 25 years previously he read a death bed confession of a fellow pris-

Sergeant John Nott of the Devon Constabulary who arrested John Lee ▶

oner, a carpenter, detailed to attend to the trap. He confessed he told John Lee to stand on the middle board as he would make that one board warp, so that when his weight was on it this one board would straighten out sufficiently to jam. The letter finishes with a postscript: 'according to what I read, the two men agreed that John Lee should say on the morning of his execution that he had a dream that night that he should not be hanged.'

A contemporary eye-witness newspaper report described Lee as walking almost unconcernedly to the scaffold and placing himself upon it without hesitation and with almost military precision and went on to say that the more force that was brought to bear, the more unyielding the trap became.

If this is the true explanation, Lee must have had nerves of iron to place his deliverance on one warped board.

The truth of the whole strange sequence of events will probably never be known. But certain facts point to a murderer other than John Lee, someone for whom he was prepared to cover up. A cryptic cutting from a Torquay newspaper of 1936, although irritatingly vague, is worth repeating.

Following the death in 1936 of Isadore Carter, Miss Keyse's solicitor who had figured prominently in Lee's arrest and trial, the story of the murder was retold but with this addition: sometime in the 1890s two young boys stood beside their father watching a coffin lowered into a grave containing the body of a demented young man of gentle birth. The father said 'Today we have buried the secret of the Babbacombe Murder.' Was the father Carter? Why were the two boys there, and why did the father make the remark, unless it was in the nature of a confession? In which churchyard did this strange scene take place? And who was the young man? Could he have been the father of Elizabeth Harris' child? And did he visit her late that night and was he disturbed by Miss Keyse? Was Lee persuaded by his step-sister to attempt to burn the body and the house, perhaps in the hope of a reward from the young man's family? When the plan failed, did Lee find himself trapped by events, or had he been set up to take the blame, perhaps consoled by the promise of large sums of money and the knowledge that his powerful confederates would somehow arrange that he should not hang?

John Lee, after his release, married a local girl and left the district some years later. The rest of his life, as with so much that went before, is a mystery, but perhaps somewhere at the back of an old drawer, or locked away with family papers, or lodged in a solicitor's office, lies a document that will at last unravel the secrets of John Lee and the Babbacombe murder.

Yeo Vale
A Mysterious Devon House

Home to most of us is the place we love best.

However humble, we cherish our homes. It is a strange man indeed who can walk away from an old and beautiful house he has lived in for ten years and vow that never again shall anyone live there and that it shall remain empty until it crumbles. Yet that was the fate of Yeo Vale House, in the parish of Alwington, on the North Devon coast. It had a history going back to the fifteenth century and beyond and had been owned by well-respected North Devon families, whose members had been magistrates, Justices of the Peace, Members of Parliament and officers of the local militia.

By the early 1900s it had come down in the world and after the First World War Yeo Vale became a country club with a shady reputation locally. Later it was sold and the last owner, Stephen Berrold, moved in around 1928 with his wife, a Persian chauffeur and two coloured female servants. To the local country folk Berrold and his household were a constant, and largely unsolved, mystery. He was well off, but not even his trusted house servants ever knew where his wealth came from. He went away for long periods, sometimes to London, sometimes abroad, but no-one knew what his business was. A light was often seen burning in his room late into the night, and he was fond of nocturnal walks. Many dubbed him a foreign spy, but there seems no justification for this — his strange habits, foreign trips and mysterious journeys in his own monoplane kept a few miles from his home at Stibb Cross being the only 'evidence'. Perhaps his 'strangeness' lay in an over-riding desire for privacy and, as they say in that part of the world, 'keeping himself to

'One morning in 1938 Stephen Berrold locked the front door and drove off, never to return.' ▶

The staff at Yeo Vale

himself'. The coloured servant girls soon left and were replaced with local staff, some of whom still live in the locality and remember Berrold and his wife.

Mrs Laura Smalldon worked at Yeo Vale as a housemaid. To her Berrold was a reasonable employer, though moody and with occasional outbursts of violent temper. She remembers Mrs Berrold as a sweet woman who was terrified of her husband. He seems to have had something of a Jekyll and Hyde character. At Christmas he gave a large party for the local children, handing out presents all round, but he would never entertain or mix with the local gentry from whom he kept himself apart. His staff seem to have been content and well treated, and Mrs Smalldon is not the only one who remembers being taken up for a flight in her employer's aeroplane — a rare enough possession today for even the most travelled businessman but almost unheard of in the 1930s.

There seemed no reason to suppose that life at Yeo Vale would not continue in its pattern for many years. But it was not to be.

When Berrold bought Yeo Vale, most of the surrounding land, once part of the estate, was owned by a neighbouring farmer called Westaway. Although he was not prepared to sell back any of the land as Berrold would have liked, farmer and country house owner got on well enough. The farm supplied dairy produce and farm goods and Berrold came to an arrangement with Farmer Westaway that no trees would be felled without prior consultation and that he would pay £30 a year for the use of the woods. It was through these woods that Berrold laid out a walk and where he often strolled at night.

Then came the row. Berrold returned from one of his frequent absences to find some of the trees had been felled. The details of the fight between the two men are no longer remembered, only the dramatic and drastic result. Stephen Berrold wanted nothing further to do with Yeo Vale, nothing further to do with the Westaways. More than that — he wanted to ensure that they would be permanently deprived of the not inconsiderable income derived from the large household they had supplied from their farm.

Despite his wife's liking for the house, Berrold decided to move. He bought another large property, Stodham Park, near Petersfield in Hampshire, and persuaded several of the local staff to move with him. All the land was sold off to within three feet of the house walls and then, one morning in 1938, Stephen Berrold locked the front door and drove off, never to return. Behind him he left an empty, silent house, doomed to decay.

The Devon servants did not remain in Hampshire for very long and within six months were back home again. Mrs Berrold who was in her early sixties, had died quite suddenly. Frank Daniels, the gardener who went briefly to Hampshire, remembers Berrold's bizarre behaviour following his wife's death. He had all her clothes packed into her car and ordered the chauffeur to drive it over the edge of the cliffs. When, understandably, he refused, Berrold set fire to the car and its contents and buried the remains in a large pit dug in the garden. His wife's ashes he kept by him, even placing them on the pillow beside him at night.

After their return to Devon, news reached the Daniels that Berrold had married a French lady and gone to live in Africa, where apparently he died some years later. He had no children, and no relatives that his servants ever knew about. But if Stephen Berrold had an heir, then he is to this day the owner of the ground on which Yeo Vale House once stood.

The loss of the house, a listed building, was a tragedy. Parts of it, in particular the central stone tower, were said to date from the fifteenth century. The flanking wings with their attractive gothic windows were described as eighteenth century. Few photographs remain of the house. It was not large, but rambled and the rear was a hotch-potch of lean-tos and additions. For many years passers-by watched with sadness its gradual decay from a once proud and beautiful manor house to a crumbling ruin.

Eventually the Westaway family bought the land, and in 1962 converted the former stabling and outbuildings at the back of the old house into their farmhouse. They had little cause to cherish Yeo Vale and its memories and saw no reason why the mouldering ruin

Yeo Vale: '. . . the loss of the house, a listed building, was a tragedy.'

The gates of Yeo Vale today . . . the house backed onto these outbuildings.

should not be put to some use. The gothic windows were removed and at hay harvest it was a familiar sight to see a conveyor belt carrying bales to the upper floor for storage. Calves were reared in the kitchen, pigs in the library, and poultry kept anywhere they could find a home. But the old house was too close for comfort and the long years of neglect had taken their toll. One chimney blew down in a gale, the floorboards were rotting and the roof beginning to leak. The stored grain attracted vermin who found the three foot gap from the farmhouse no barrier at all.

But local children used it as a playground and Mr John Westaway, son of the original farmer with whom Berrold had his row, foresaw that one day there would be a tragedy if he did not act. He applied for permission to demolish. It was a listed building, but now Berrold was dead who was the owner? Who was responsible for its maintenance? The local council could not afford to take on so onerous a task and in 1973 the final blow fell and Yeo Vale was bull-dozed. Within a few hours centuries of history were reduced to a pile

Above:
Mr and Mrs Berrold
Right:
The staircase at Yeo Vale

of rubble. Mr Westaway, who had insured himself against the appearance of an heir to claim the vanished house, broke even on the deal. The cost of demolition was £1,000 and the contractor bought the rubble from him — for £1,000.

The area was levelled by the local council who were carrying out some roadworks locally and found the site convenient for tipping their waste.

All that survives are the Westaways home, the former walled gardens, the kennels where Berrold kept his greyhounds, a weir in the river used to generate electricity, a rapidly decaying chapel in the woods — and the wrought iron entrance gates, sturdy but rusting, that today open on to nothing but a grass field.

The Great Trick

The Romany people call it the *hokkani boro*—the great trick—and many a poor person must have been cheated of their life's savings when countryfolk were both more superstitious and simple than they are today. The trick involved much mumbo-jumbo and a quick substitution. Working on the greed of a gullible person, the gypsy would persuade them to place all their money wrapped in an old cloth, or half the gypsy's scarf, in a secret hiding place, convinced that after some weeks it would miraculously have doubled or trebled in quantity. Whilst uttering spells and charms over the money, the gypsy would swop the bundle of money for a similar bundle of stones—and by the time the deception was discovered he would be many miles away.

Today we would call it a confidence trick and laugh that anyone could be so simple as to fall for it. But in Plymouth in 1936 a doctor was tricked out of £2,300 by a not dissimilar method.

Three men were involved, who were only brought to trial after much patient police work and not a little luck. Hyman Kurasch, then 52, and considered the mastermind, is now dead, as is Jack Carter, but the third may still be alive. Under the Rehabilitation of Offenders Act we cannot reveal his identity. Time, according to this law, has expiated his crime. Therefore we will call him 'Sammy'. We can, however, tell you that he is a Londoner and played a major part in this modern version of the Great Trick.

Kurasch, no doubt wished he had never chosen Plymouth for the scene of his last trick. How many times he had previously successfully pulled it off will never be known as pride probably prevented many of his victims ever coming forward. Whilst searching for a suitable victim, he stayed at the Farley Hotel in Union Street, demolished as a result of the wartime blitzes. Sammy had lodgings near Millbay Docks, and Carter was busy establishing an

alibi in the Cheshire village of High Lane.

Kruger sovereigns, worth much more than their face value, were the bait and Dr Albert Bradlaw was the victim. Sammy visited his surgery in the Beacon Park area of Plymouth for some cough medicine. Speaking in a broken English accent he proffered one Kruger sovereign taken from a cement pill box in payment of the five shilling bill. Dr Bradlaw bit. He took the coin and asked Sammy to return the next day for his change. By the time Sammy returned with Carter, the doctor had checked on the value of the sovereign and he was more than interested in the two men's tale of how they had smuggled over 2,000 of these sovereigns out of Germany in cement pill boxes. For £2,300 the doctor agreed to purchase them. Next day Carter and Sammy brought with them a carpet bag full of pill boxes, some of which they opened and showed to the doctor, containing the Kruger sovereigns. The £2,300 was counted, wrapped in a red handkerchief and it was agreed that this should be placed in the carpet bag and the bag locked up in the doctor's safe whilst the two men fetched the balance of the sovereigns. This was done, the men left, and the doctor waited. And waited.

Although he had carefully watched whilst the money was placed in the bag, and the bag closed and put in the safe, he became suspicious. The *hokkani boro* had worked yet again—the red handkerchief contained scraps of paper and the cement pill boxes contained nothing at all.

Solving the crime and bringing the three men to justice was in itself almost as mystical as the trick. Hyman Kurasch was connected with the crime only because the head of CID, Detective Sergeant W. T. Bill Hutchings had a long memory. He recalled a similar trick being worked on the Continent when the police suspected Kurasch although he was never arrested. But his description fitted neither of Dr Bradlaw's two visitors. How many master criminals are eventually caught because of a stupid piece of carelessness? Kurasch left Plymouth without paying his bill at the Farley Hotel, where he had stayed under the name of Curry. The hotel identified Kurasch from a photo and Bill Hutchings called in Scotland Yard who circulated rumours in London's underworld that 'Hymie' was wanted in Plymouth for the petty crime of not paying his hotel

◄**Author, Michael Williams**

81

bill. Was it pride, or a desire to gloat, that prompted Kurasch to return in person to pay that bill? The police were waiting and he was arrested.

But the doctor had never seen Kurasch and there was nothing to connect him with the crime. Bail was fixed at £1,000 and here Bill Hutchings had his second stroke of luck. The money was paid to him by a local boxer well known to the detective. During questioning the boxer admitted that the £1,000 was not his but had been given to him by an unknown man to stand surety for Kurasch. This was illegal, so the money was impounded and bail refused.

Routine police work revealed Sammy's lodgings—and a fragment of cement in his room. His photograph was circulated. But who was his accomplice? Again Bill Hutchings' memory recalled a man called Carter, known to have worked with Sammy, a confidence-trick and sleight-of-hand expert. Descriptions sent to all police stations uncovered Carter's connection with High Lane—and his alibi. But Hutchings backed his hunch and had Carter arrested and brought to Plymouth, where the doctor identified him. But still there was nothing to link Kurasch with the crime, and Sammy remained at liberty. Modern police methods involving computers and high technology are far in advance of resources in the 1930s, but we doubt whether they could have solved this crime. Computers do not use hunches, or dishes of bananas and cream.

Bill Hutchings, in an attempt to gain information, talked to Jack Carter every evening—friendly, cosy informal chats. But Carter would not break the criminal code. His wife knew nothing of her husband's underworld activities but she did confide in the detective that she always gave him bananas and cream on his birthday. Was it luck that Carter's sixtieth birthday was that week? Touched by the gesture of his birthday treat, Carter parted with just one piece of information—an address in King's Cross used by Hymie Kurasch. The flat was raided and one of the men, Detective Sergeant Hare, played a prominent part in bringing in the guilty verdict.

Sammy, too, had been arrested and the three stood trial in January, 1937. Carter and Sammy pleaded guilty, but the evidence against Kurasch was painfully slender. As in the past he had covered his tracks all too well. Because he had pleaded 'Not Guilty' and his connection with the crime was not obvious, a legal wrangle followed as to whether Detective Sergeant Hare's evidence was admissible. As long as Hare answered only those questions permitted by the Recorder he was allowed into the witness box. The process of question, followed by consideration by the Recorder, and answer, was slow and tedious. Hare must have found it monotonous and surely could be forgiven for forgetting to wait for approval before replying to the question 'What did you find in Kurasch's flat?' His answer, just three words, almost certainly tipped the scales against Kurasch. 'Nine Kruger sovereigns,' Hare replied. He was reprimanded and ordered to leave the box, but the damage was done.

A criminal, with an international record, was finally brought to justice in Plymouth; Kurasch went to prison for five years. Carter was sentenced to three years, and Sammy to eighteen months' hard labour.

The poor doctor never recovered his lost £2,300 but after one or two unsuccessful claims for the £1,000 impounded bail money, this was awarded to him by way of compensation.

Some Strange Devon Happenings

Below Clovelly Dykes as the land falls to the sea is a quiet undisturbed area of woodland, adjacent to the hustle and bustle of popular Clovelly, but set apart and rarely visited. Here the oaks grow closely, twisted and misshapen by the cruel westerly winds and here must surely be some of the first oaks ever to grow on Devon soil — some of the ancient, original woodland.

Hidden amongst these trees is a simple, wooden cross. It marks the place where, 'after three weeks' search, the bodies of Eliza Lee, aged 11, and Ellen Lee, aged two years, were found on November 19 1862'.

The two little girls went missing one Saturday afternoon. They had gone to collect wood and were last seen by a ploughman at five o'clock asleep under a hedge. The sisters had earlier spent some time watching him plough. He roused them and without a word they appeared to obey his instructions to go home, back to Clovelly. Did they halt for a rest and fall asleep again, succumbing to the November cold, or did they hide in fear from the darkness that had overtaken them in the woods?

Despite an extensive search by five policemen and most of the parish, it was three weeks before the bodies were discovered, only fifty feet from the track.

At the inquest it was stated that their clothes were torn and their legs and arms scratched, but there were no signs of violence. Despite a newspaper report condemning the mother's 'astonishing indifference to the children's plight', no-one came forward with tales of cruelty or hardship and the children appeared well-fed, although the elder had run away before.

Hidden amongst the trees is a simple wooden cross, marking the strange death of two children. ▶

84

A verdict of death due to exposure was brought in, and ever since they have been known as the 'babes in the wood'.

For many years the woodlands were neglected; the undergrowth became an impenetrable tangle and the track was all but lost.

Few remembered the children or could have taken you to the cross. In 1971 the Forestry Commission, who now 'manage' the woodland, stumbled on the forgotten memorial and cleared the encroaching foliage. Wisely they have left it hidden among the trees, but it is still there for those who know where to look.

Not far away—across the valley from the cross is a very old house, half hidden amongst the trees. There has been a dwelling there since the twelfth century but the present building is quite modern, only about three hundred years old. It is called Velly, and has been the home of Mrs Frances Clark since she was seven. She is now 85.

The windows of the house look out over the woodland to the sea — the best view in the world, Mrs Clark calls it, and so deep is her love for her home she is not at all surprised that a former owner, long

Velly House: 'Local servants had often seen the cavalier who walked in through the back door.'

dead, should want to return again and again. She has never seen the ghost, but is aware of his frequent visits, and knows quite well who he is.

Local servants had often seen the cavalier who walked in through the back door and described him to her when, as a child, she first became aware of his presence.

Above the south door in Hartland's parish church at Stoke is a very old memorial. The lettering is now faint, but it is just possible to read that it commemorates 'John Velly, who faithfully served that glorious Prince Charles the Martyr, and his son, during the civil wars as a "Captain Lewtenant" to Sir Robert Cary,' and died in 1694.

Mrs Clark believes this is the identity of her ghost, whose benign presence has kept her company through many long evenings. But it is as well he fought on the right side in the Civil War for had he been a Cromwellian, Mrs Clark says she could not have lived with him!

★ ★ ★ ★ ★

Parts of Devon — like parts of Cornwall — have a haunted, haunting quality. Material and mystical, past and present all somehow merge and maybe an isolated sense of geography comes into it. Superstition too is often only just below the surface.

Anyway we decided to investigate some strange happenings in the county.

Our next account came from a young West of England journalist Alan McKinley, based near Tavistock. This is what he told us.

'Chasing a UFO in a two-door, 800 cc Honda Civic is undoubtedly undertaken by, you would think, optimists or nutters. But I consider myself to be neither, and my two friends who shared such an experience don't really fall into those categories either. But, as Julie Andrews says, let's start at the very beginning.

'On a cold November night I and two friends were returning from Plymouth to Tavistock. I don't think we had been to see *Close Encounters* that evening but perhaps it would explain a lot. Anyway on our way back on the A386 just past Roborough we all saw a greenish haze in the sky towards the west. And we could make out flashing lights moving towards it which we presumed were aeroplane lights. We didn't bother to ponder on the meaning of the lights as journalists are a notoriously cynical bunch. But when a man in what appeared to be a grey Air Force uniform waved us down just after Bedford Bridge — together with a few other cars — our professional collective curiosity was aroused. He told us the road was closed and we'd have to find another way into town. He would not elaborate on the reasons for this except to say the road was blocked. We could not make out what uniform he was wearing, but it was not police.

'Only one of us lived in Tavistock so we decided to abandon the taxi service and go to my house in Buckland Monachorum. But as we got nearer to Buck, we could see the lights again, with what appeared to be a large number of car headlights moving towards

'Parts of Devon have a haunted, haunting quality . . .'

them. Secret defence manoeuvres? A good story we thought.

'Off we went to get closer, stopping from time to time to check our bearings — Devon hedges were not made with navigation in mind. We could see other lights now as we clambered onto the car to see over the hedges around Buckland, but these were red and airborne, and the cluster of lights shone as brightly as before.

'As well as being bad for visibility, the roads around Buckland are nothing like straight and we didn't know the area too well, so we lost our bearings once or twice and lost sight of the lights. But if all else failed we could still make our way back to where we had a fair view of the lights.

'About an hour after we had first seen the lights we lost them. We even went back to the original place we saw them, but all was dark, except for the moonlight, and quiet.

'Although the three of us were journalists, and much puzzled, frightened and fascinated at what we saw, we were very tired journalists, and it was 2 a.m. We didn't know where to go or how to get there, so we abandoned the search.

'I don't believe in UFOs, and neither do my friends. We all believe there is a logical, believable and harmless explanation for what we saw that night.

'We just have no idea what it is.'

The verdict of those journalists reminded us of something Judy Chard wrote in her book *Devon Mysteries:*

'I don't think hauntings just occur — I think some particular physical presence is needed to cause an apparition to appear. Maybe there are people who attract the past in some way so that exorcism, if it is practised, has its effect on the people at the place and not on the supposed spirits. As a water diviner I know everthing has its "field" or aura, so perhaps evil or good can impress itself and cause this atmosphere that many people feel. Some buildings seem to oppress us with a sense of the people who have lived and died in them. It isn't so very hard to understand, for the walls and floors and ceilings of old buildings must be saturated with the exhalations of human emotions. I read somewhere the theory that a shadow that once falls on a wall leaves a shadow there forever.

'To be honest I have seen neither ghost nor UFO, neither do I know how water divining occurs although I can dowse in a very amateur way, neither do I understand how a coloured picture is brought to my room from thousands of miles away by satellite — so

I shall repeat the well worn quotation that "there are more things in heaven and earth, Horatio, than are dreamed of in your philosophy."

★ ★ ★ ★ ★

Our trail for strange happenings next took us to Grenofen Manor, a country club nestling in beautifully wooded grounds, alongside the River Walkham, just outside Tavistock. Once more Sally Dodd of *The Tavistock Times* had done some detective work for us. 'Go and see Sue Perryman,' she advised.

Sue and Bob Perryman took over this listed building a while back — it was known as the old Gentry House and the original Elizabethan manor dates back to the twelfth century — it was in a near-ruinous condition. They are now painstakingly rebuilding and reshaping the property.

Sue Perryman, who has those blue eyes that you associate with psychic people, talked in the lounge which was the servants' quarters in the old days — the massive granite fireplace with logs burning is a relic of those times.

'When we first came here,' she explained, 'we were told by different people that there was a ghost in this building, and before we started renovating neither of us believed it, and always passed it off . . . Bob doesn't really believe in that sort of thing. Anyway, one evening, I came across to open up on my own and was in the bar slicing lemon when I turned to pick up the ice bucket . . . and saw a long length of ash in the ashtray. I thought, "Maybe the last customer last night may have said 'Good Night' on his way out and flicked ash into the clean ash tray as he went out." We always make a rule of cleaning all the ash trays last thing at night and all the others were clean.

'About three weeks later I went to open the bar, again on my own, and I thought about what had happened on the previous occasion. So I checked all the ash trays on the bar . . . and they were all clean . . . well, I sliced up the lemons and turned to pick up the ice bucket.

'Sue Perryman: ' . . . we hear the lounge door bang . . . which it shouldn't because it's always locked when we're closed.' ▶

And suddenly I saw ash in the ash tray! Now though I do smoke, I can assure you I hadn't lit up!

'Then, about two months later, I opened up, again on my own, once more I was in the bar slicing lemon, when I heard the back door open and close. I thought it was the "door man"; he always walks through the lounge to the main entrance. I was still in the bar and kept looking out for him to give him the float money for the entrance till. When I realized it wasn't him, I decided it must have been one of the kitchen staff who had gone straight into the kitchen. I picked up the ice bucket and went through towards the kitchen . . . when I reached the kitchen, the door was still locked . . . and I was still on my own!

'Later on, one Sunday morning, there were three of us cleaning up. The hot water in the lounge takes ages to come through . . . and I turned it on and went into the cellar and had a word with Liza. While chatting to her, I could *see* Joe, the third member of our party . . . when we finished nattering I went out into the passage and as I walked towards the lounge I could hear a tap running in one of the staff loos. I looked in and the cold tap was on full pelt. I asked Liza "Have you had this tap on?" "No," she said, "funny." We shrugged it off, and I went back to the tap I had left running in the lounge . . . and it was turned off! And it wasn't any of us who had done it . . . and nobody else had been inside the building.

'Since then we have moved to a flat above the premises and very often when in bed we hear the lounge door bang . . . which it shouldn't because it's *always* locked when we're closed. My brother-in-law stayed with us to help complete our function room. One morning he came into breakfast and asked if we had left the door open because he had heard it banging in the night . . . and we hadn't mentioned any of the earlier incidents.

'"He" or whatever it is, plays Hell with the tills. I can take a till reading at the end of the day and know that what's rung up is impossible. One of my barmaids hates working in the lounge because she says she gets "weird shivers" and goes "cold" despite the fact that it's a lovely warm room. She can be wearing a blouse and cardigan and still feel like ice. Another barmaid wore a bracelet, which she'd just had repaired, and it flew off. She won't wear it here again.

'A friend of ours from London, called Terry, came down to install the sound system. He was a total disbeliever on the subject of the

Supernatural. Well, he was fixing the system and thought he saw someone pass by from the corner of his eye . . . he really thought he saw someone go across in front of him. My daughter had a friend staying with us and he thought they were playing a trick. So he decided to catch them out and nipped round the other way to catch up with them there but there wasn't a soul about.

'Joe, our cleaner, is always calling out, "Who's there?" I think I see someone go past the main entrance and Joe very often does. We go out to look . . . but no-one's there.'

Reg Pearce, another member of the club's staff, supports Sue Perryman's feelings despite an initial scepticism. 'I had never believed in the Supernatural,' he said, 'frankly I'd always considered it a load of codswollop. But my views have changed somewhat since coming to work at Grenofen Manor. One morning in September 1981 I arrived to clean the beer lines. I obtained the keys to the club and unlocked . . . there was a tap running in the staff toilet. I asked the plumber, who was working in the function room, if he had turned it on . . . he said "No" . . . nor had anybody else.

'Then in the October I arrived at eight o'clock and unlocked the club . . . all the doors were unlocked and shut when I went to light the fire in the lounge . . . suddenly there was the sound of a door slamming. I went to check and found the doors exactly as I had left them. . . I checked outside too but nobody was about. I came back in and checked the fire, shutting all the doors behind me. I then felt the air change and go cold because on walking back to the bar I found the access door, *which I had shut,* open! That made the hair on my neck bristle . . . I shut the door again but felt uncomfortable . . . I cannot properly explain it but I felt I was not alone . . . so now I do not know.'

Now these accounts taken individually may not mean much — no ghost in three-cornered hat, no clanging chains — but taken collectively they represent a Supernatural 'something'. Moreover all the versions are matter-of-fact — possibly even a little lightweight — nevertheless we think they're worthy of inclusion, and we shall keep in touch with Sue Perryman about future happenings at the Manor. Our instinct is that the story could only be unfolding.

★ ★ ★ ★ ★

The fifteenth century church at Oare which R.D. Blackmore made the setting for the marriage of Lorna Doone

Can there be such a thing as total fiction?

We doubt it, especially after visiting Chagford.

R. D. Blackmore in his famous Westcountry novel *Lorna Doone*, first published in 1869, wrote how Lorna was shot on her wedding day. 'Darling eyes, the clearest eyes, the loveliest, the most loving eyes—the sound of a shot rang through the church, and those eyes were dim with death.'

We can only guess that Blackmore might have known about a factual incident here around 1641 when Mary Whiddon was shot dead by a jealous lover while she was being married to another man at the very altar of the Church of St Michael in Chagford.

Or was it an uncanny coincidence that fact and fiction ran a parallel path? Now, of course, we shall never know.

Just outside Chagford stands Whiddon Park, a grand old house, mentioned in Peter Underwood's fascinating *Ghosts of Devon*. 'In August 1971 the daughter of the house was married at Chagford Church. On the morning of the wedding a guest at Whiddon Park found himself wide awake in the half light of early morning and he saw the form of a young woman in an old-fashioned wedding dress standing in the doorway.'

So maybe the sad ghost of Mary Whiddon still haunts this corner of Devon.

Moreover Chagford has yet another ghost. He is Sydney Godolphin, a Cavalier and poet, who haunts that lovely mullioned and gabled inn, The Three Crowns, just across the road from the Church of St Michael's. Elected a Member of Parliament at the age of eighteen, a close friend of Ben Johnson, Sydney Godolphin's loyalty to King Charles cost him his life. He was seriously wounded in a skirmish with the Parliamentarians — hit in the leg by a musket ball — and died soon afterwards laid out on that stone bench in the doorway of The Three Crowns.

A number of people claim to have heard his ghostly footsteps pacing the corridor of the inn — and some even claim to have seen his ghost.

There's an interesting link too with sad Mary Whiddon because an ancestor of hers, John Whiddon, a Judge of the King's Bench in London, had this place built as a manor house in the thirteenth century.

As we said, we seriously doubt whether there can be such a thing as complete myth.

Left: 'Mary Whiddon was shot dead by a jealous lover . . . at the very altar of the Church of St Michael in Chagford.'
Below: The Three Crowns, Chagford: '. . . another ghost. He is Sydney Godolphin, a Cavalier and poet, who haunts the inn.'

'Maybe the hidden woods of Dartmoor are home to more wild
animals than is realised . . .'

Nor do we think the stories of the Black Dog should be dismissed as pure fiction. Though the people of Devon are well known for their reluctance to talk about strange happenings and to outsiders will normally deny all knowledge of anything remotely supernatural. Rumours of the Black Dog have persisted for hundreds of years. The dog, of huge size, is not peculiar to Devon — East Anglia boasts a similar animal as do parts of Dorset. Its origins are unknown but the dog does not appear sinister and Devonians of past generations accepted its presence without fear. Sightings seem most common on long straight stretches of road, especially ancient tracks.

Amongst the many who have seen the black dog but feared to talk lest they were laughed at is Mr William Nott of Barnstaple. He would have kept his story secret but for one fact — he had three witnesses.

Mr Nott was for many years a bus driver in North Devon. On Christmas Eve in 1939 he left Barnstaple at around 5.40 in the morning bound for Lynton. With him were a soldier going home on leave, the head waiter of a Lynton hotel, and his conductor, Mr Ruddall. It was a beautiful morning with a huge moon and the countryside was so clearly illuminated it reminded Mr Nott of the line 'all silvered o'er with light' from one of Schubert's songs.

Suddenly ahead of him on the previously empty road he saw a huge black dog and three sheep. The dog turned in front of the bus and although he stood on his brakes and pulled on the handbrake, Mr Nott expected a sickening thud. Nothing happened and when he jumped out there was no sign of either the dog or the sheep. To his relief, the conductor joined Mr Nott and asked him what had happened to the animals.

Both men walked to the rear of the bus where the soldier was standing in the road, also looking for the sheep and the dog. And the head waiter, still inside the bus, agreed that they had indeed very nearly run over one large black dog and three sheep.

Mr Nott and his conductor examined the steep banks on either side of the road but there was no means of escape and the only explanation was that the animals had vanished into thin air. The dog was about the size of a Great Dane, but Mr Nott had no time to notice anything else about it.

The incident took place as the bus was approaching Blackmoor Gate, and once the story got about Mr Nott was told of several other sightings of the black dog in that area. He was told of a farmer who, travelling very late one night near South Molton, suddenly found himself surrounded by a flock of sheep being herded by a black dog. Just as suddenly they all disappeared and he was alone again in the middle of an empty field.

Unrelated stories of sightings occur all over Devon but in the 1930s Mrs Barbara Carbonell attempted to trace a definite route from Coplestone in mid Devon to Weare Giffard and the coast in North Devon. Born in Bideford, she later moved to Bow and is remembered as a keen local historian. Despite the usual local reticence, Mrs Carbonell achieved some success. Her route began at a cross roads near Coplestone where an ancient cross still marks the resting place of a bishop's coffin, and followed the old drove road from North Devon to Exeter before the turnpike was built. Several villagers talked of the creature that raced through Down St Mary at night. None would admit to seeing the dog, but said his panting could be clearly heard, as could the sound of the schoolhouse wall being knocked down in the beast's haste.

From this village to Stopgate Cross the road coincides with an ancient track and Mrs Carbonell talked to a driver who had on many occasions seen the black dog. He admitted that at first he was scared but when he realised the animal meant no harm he and his two horses became accustomed to the huge dog as he accompanied them down the track. Winkleigh aerodrome obliterated the old roads and the next recorded sightings were in the parish of St Giles, near Torrington. Here a few villagers did admit to seeing the dog themselves and hearing tales of other sightings. Mrs Carbonell's researches were brought up to date by her own daughter who, whilst on a visit to her mother then living outside Bideford, was returning from Winkleigh late one night. The next morning she told her mother that as they drove along the road from Torrington at a point below Frithelstock Priory, a large black dog crossed in front of them. Her husband stopped so suddenly he stalled the car and both were certain that the animal had been hit. But the dog had completely disappeared. When shown the exact spot, Mrs Carbonell realised it was in direct line with her mystical route.

More recently, sightings of a strange black cat-like animal have been reported around the fringes of Dartmoor. Attempts are being made to prove that some mysterious leopard-like creature is at large and that the hidden woods of Dartmoor are home to more wild animals than is generally realised. One naturalist claims to have seen

100

tracks belonging to members of the big cat family and to have heard and smelt them in the woods at night. Others who have seen unidentified large black beasts include policemen and firemen, a lorry driver who saw a strange animal on two consecutive nights, and a boy and his dog, both of whom turned tail and ran.

The prosaic members of the population are in a quandary — is it more likely that at some time a black leopard or puma has escaped and is roaming and breeding in remote areas, although such an escape has never been reported? Or are all these separate incidents modern sightings of that strange phenomena which has haunted the Devon countryside for centuries — the mysterious Black Dog?

Acknowledgments

We are indebted to all the people who gave interviews and allowed us to quote them — and those who lent photographs. We are also grateful to David & Charles for letting us quote an extract from *Sabine Baring-Gould* by Bickford H.C. Dickinson, Rufus Endle for providing detailed background information on a Plymouth crime, and Sally Dodd who gave us some invaluable leads. Finally a personal 'thank you' to Brenda Duxbury for her careful editing.

ALSO AVAILABLE

STRANGE HAPPENINGS IN CORNWALL

by Michael Williams. 35 photographs.

Strange shapes and strange characters; healing and life after death; reincarnation and Spiritualism; murders and mysteries are only some of the contents in this fascinating book.

'... this eerie Cornish collection.'

David Foot, Western Daily Press

OCCULT IN THE WEST

by Michael Williams. Over 30 photographs.

Michael Williams follows his successful *Supernatural in Cornwall* with further interviews and investigations into the Occult — this time incorporating Devon. Ghosts and clairvoyancy, dreams and psychic painting, healing and hypnosis are only some of the facets of a fascinating story.

'... provides the doubters with much food for thought.'

Jean Kenzie, Tavistock Gazette

DEVON MYSTERIES

by Judy Chard. 22 photographs.

Devon is not only a beautiful county, it's a mysterious place too — and if anybody had any doubts about that, Judy Chard demolishes them with her exploration into the strange and often the inexplicable. This book, though, is not just about *mysterious Devon*, it's essentially about *Devon mysteries*.

'... my appetite for unexplained happenings has been truly whetted by Newton Abbot author Judy Chard's latest offering.'   Mid Devon Advertiser

'... comprehensive catalogue of strange goings-on in Devon ...'

North Devon Journal-Herald

LEGENDS OF DEVON

by Sally Jones. 60 photographs and drawings.

Devon is a mine of folklore and myth. Here in a journey through legendary Devon, Sally Jones brings into focus some fascinating tales, showing us that the line dividing fact and legend is an intriguing one.

'...Sally Jones has trodden the path of legendary Devon well...'

Tavistock Times

CORNISH MYSTERIES

by Michael Williams. 40 photographs.

Cornish Mysteries is a kind of jig-saw puzzle in words and pictures. The power of charming, mysterious shapes in the Cornish landscape, the baffling murder case of Mrs Hearn are just some fascinating ingredients.

'... superstitions, dreams, murder, Lyonesse, the legendary visit of the boy Jesus to Cornwall, and much else. Splendid, and sometimes eerie, chapters.'

The Methodist Recorder

OTHER BOSSINEY TITLES INCLUDE

SUPERNATURAL IN CORNWALL
by Michael Williams

MY DEVON

LUNDY ISLAND
by Joan Rendell

ALONG THE LEMON
by Judy Chard

MY DARTMOOR
by Clive Gunnell

FOLLOWING THE TAMAR
by Sarah Foot

MY GRANDFATHER ISAAC FOOT
by Sarah Foot

ALONG THE TEIGN
by Judy Chard

ABOUT WIDECOMBE
by Judy Chard

THE SOUTH HAMS
by Judy Chard

THE BARBICAN
by Elizabeth Gunnell

THE PLYMOUTH BLITZ
by Frank Wintle

DARTMOOR PRISON
by Rufus Endle

TO TAVISTOCK GOOSIE FAIR
by Clive Gunnell